Odense University Slavic Studies vol. 10

Soviet Civilization between Past and Present

Soviet Civilization between Past and Present

Edited by
Mette Bryld & Erik Kulavig

Odense University Press 1998

The publication of *Soviet Civilization between Past and Present* was made possible by a grant from Odense University on the recommendation of Professor Bent Jensen and Professor Aage Trommer.

© The editors and Odense University Press 1998
Typographical layout by DTP-Funktionen, Odense University
Cover design by Ulla Poulsen Precht
Printed by Olesen Offset, Viborg, Denmark
ISBN 87 7838 330 7
ISSN 0078 3277

Cover illustrations: the erection of marshal Zhukov and the downfall of cosmonaut Gagarin (photos taken 1995 in Moscow by Mette Bryld).

Odense University Press
Campusvej 55
DK-5230 Odense M

Phone +45 66 15 79 99
Fax +45 66 15 81 26
E-mail: press@forlag.ou.dk
Internet-location: http://www.ou.dk/press

Contents

Mette Bryld
Introduction — 7

Ol'ga Velikanova
The Function of Lenin's Image
in Soviet Mass Consciousness — 13

Irina Sandomirskaya
Proletarian Tourism:
Incorporated History and Incorporated Rhetoric — 39

Mette Bryld
The Days of Dogs and Dolphins:
Aesopian Metaphors of Soviet Science — 53

Erik Kulavig
Evidence of Public Dissent in the Khrushchev Years — 77

Natal'ia Kozlova
On the Cognitive-Normative Mapping of Soviet Civilization:
The Space Beneath — 95

Søren Damkjaer
The Body and Cultural Transition in Russia — 115

David Gillespie and Natal'ia Zhuravkina
National Identity and the Past in Recent Russian Cinema — 133

Hans Henrik Brockdorff
The Individual and the Collective:
A Cultural Approach to the Question
of Dualism in Soviet Society   147

Pernille Larsen
Transition in Practice:
Political Discourse and Market Patterns
in Vilnius, Lithuania   165

Contributors   185

Index   187

Introduction

METTE BRYLD

Today apocalyptic visions dominate the discourses on the new Russia. A weekly paper such as *Literaturnaia gazeta*, randomly chosen on 4 December 1996, is full of articles which underpin the horror of the situation. In one of them the well-known economist, Nikolai Shmelev, foresees an imminent social upheaval which may well result in the country's disappearance from the map of the world. A famished army and huge, impoverished regions seriously threaten what little national unity may have been left, he says. Another article focuses on the terrible conditions of the marginalised lower depths of society which constitute no less than 10% of the population, or fourteen million people (about three times as many as the total population of Denmark) and which seem only to be growing. Yet a third tells how schools which in theory should be fully subsidised by the state are being forced to act against the law by squeezing huge amounts of money out of the pupils' parents just in order to function. If you cannot pay, your child may not pass the final examination and all doors except those leading to a miserable life in the army or on the streets may be closed, this true life story suggests.

The list of misery and poverty could be continued but the point is made: the materiality and embodied torments which the regimes of yesterday tried to keep out of sight through textuality have returned with a vengeance. In the new Russia harsh social realism has replaced the rosy visions of socialist realism; a dystopian no-future outlook has now superseded the former future-oriented utopianism. But just as today's Russia, according to these warning voices, may have no future, it also seems to have no past. The nostalgic eagerness with which a specific Russian history, often conspicuously coloured by Soviet aesthetics, is currently being re-invented and incorporated into orthodox churches and heroic monuments in the capital gives visible evidence of the feverish quest for national identity. The term 'the new Russia' is thus much more than a phrase. 'Russia is a country that before 1 January 1992 had never existed', D. Gillespie and N. Zhuravkina acutely state in their contribution to the present anthology. In this new nation, the geo-political space of which in many respects differs from that of the pre-revolutionary Russian Empire, 'only the cultural consciousness remains, and this is being constantly enriched and changed as "new" (in many cases forgotten and repressed) names and works (re-)enter the canon'.

Inspired by a similar point of view the editors have concentrated this collection of essays on various aspects and manifestations of consciousness, in particular of mass consciousness, in the Soviet Union and post-Soviet Russia (with a detour to Lithuania). Several of our contributors have made profitable use of recently opened archives and discovered materials which, by their efforts, are now being made available for discoursive recycling. However, whether based on archive documents or not, re-constructed fragments of cultural consciousness and social memory, hovering between the past and the present, make up the main bulk of this book.

In the opening chapter, "The Function of Lenin's Image in Soviet Mass Consciousness", Ol'ga Velikanova bonds the past with the present in demonstrating both the persistence and the transformation of the Lenin cult from its formative years until today. On the basis of formerly secret reports and summaries of the Soviet political police as well as uncensored folklore sources she shows the differences and congruences between the features of Lenin's image invented by the regime and those generated in the imagination of the masses. While the former aimed at presenting this embodiment of the Party as a political hero and role model, the latter spontaneously perceived him in traditional, pre-revolutionary images – as Saint, Protector and good Tsar. But even if these various myths have been repeatedly dismantled, Lenin is still very much 'alive'. Apart from the fact that his Mausoleum has not yet been removed from the centre of Moscow, public opinion polls show, as Velikanova reminds us, that 'about half of those queried still regard Lenin as a positive symbol'. Even today, many Russians, faithful to the desires of yesterday, have not given up their citizenship in imaginary Leninland.

The next contribution, written by Irina Sandomirskaya, turns to a 'forgotten phenomenon of early Stalinist society', namely proletarian tourism which, as she points out, became part of the Soviet ideological machine. By analysing three genres of tourism from her position as a linguist, Sandomirskaya identifies the specific type of rhetoric to which each of these genres belong. But although these 'cultural idioms' clearly belong to the inventory of Soviet ideological discourse, the very institution which organised proletarian tourism was, she observes, driven also by 'the repressed desires of individuals'. Her chapter is consequently entitled "Proletarian Tourism: Incorporated History and Incorporated Rhetoric".

Incorporated Aesopian metaphors might have been an apt title for my own contribution on "The Days of Dogs and Dolphins: Aesopian Metaphors of Soviet Science" which deals with both Soviet political discourses and the life sciences as aspects of 'story-telling practices' (Haraway 1989: 4). Animals often function as substitutes for humans and they did so very openly even in the official doctrines of the Soviet Union. In unravelling the story of Ivan Pavlov's domesticated dogs and Aleksei Yablokov's wild dolphins as gendered and humanised agents of a political-cultural context, I moreover make a bridge to Erik Kulavig's chapter on "Evidence of Public Dissent in the Khrushchev Years". The 'thaw' which entered this book on the back of matriarchal-oriented dolphins, is in Kulavig's interpretation shown as having been an active mood of dissent among broad layers of the population. The view on the Soviet people as mere passive Pavlovian dogs is here successfully contradicted. Dissent was, as Kulavig's archive materials indicate, by no means restricted to the intelligentsia alone. Protests, demonstrations and even riots were far more common at that time than has generally been thought in the West. His contribution therefore rehabilitates the Russians from the stereotyped image which portrays them as gripped by a specific "Asiatic" passivity and fatalism.

Natal'ia Kozlova's chapter "On the Cognitive-Normative Mapping of Soviet Civilization: The Space Beneath" provides an extraordinary insight into the culture of poverty which was neither researched nor mentioned in the years of Soviet power. In Kozlova's words, 'the lifestyles and social games of the lower classes seem to have been located right "in the blind spot" of Soviet vision'. Moreover, Kozlova manages to avoid the pitfalls of an objectifying and hierarchic othering since her analysis of the life of the semi-illiterate woman, E. G. Kiseleva, is based on the "diaries" of the elderly woman herself (Kiseleva started writing after 1977 when she was over sixty). The muted is given voice and a paradox speaks out – for although the 'nethermost' spaces, to which Kiseleva belonged, were ignored by the socialist regime, this woman nevertheless represented a generation of peasants which, impressed by the technological magic of industrialization, in its own way endorsed the system.

The lower depths occupied by the Kiselevas of the Soviet world by and large existed outside the bodily regimes which are the focus of Søren Damkjaer's "The Body and Cultural Transition in Russia". Reflecting on the bodies typical of various types of modernity, Damkjaer observes that the 'Soviet society developed a number of restricted and standardised forms of movement regimes according to an early modern or modern scheme'. The transition we are witnessing in Russia is therefore also a transformation or emancipation of the body. An emancipation at least from the puritanical idea of the proper Soviet body, for as Damkjaer also points out, these bodily regimes were, in fact, never internalised except in the institutions of elite sport. Like so much else in the Soviet Union they largely remained a project.

In the following two chapters, the so far downgraded sphere of artistic and literary creativity in late Soviet and post-Soviet culture comes to the fore. In their contribution, "National Identity and the Past in Recent Russian Cinema", David Gillespie and Natal'ia Zhuravkina discuss the relationship between the current search for identity and the ideologies formulated in films. The importance of their interpretations should be evident: unlike Western Europe, the two contributors rightly inform us, Russian identity is not as yet based 'on political institutions, but above all on culture, and the cultural consciousness is one which 1917 did not break'.

Culture, including the by now rehabilitated philosophical heritage, is likewise the subject of Hans Henrik Brockdorff's "The Individual and the Collective: A Cultural Approach to the Question of Dualism in Soviet Society". Focussing on a broad spectrum of manifestations of the non-official 'second culture', the underground, Brockdorff identifies some major tendencies characteristic of this out-lawed cultural stage during the 1970s and 1980s. He also takes up the new situation which emerged with the recognition of the underground by the end of the 1980s and discusses Russia's current, often bewildering cultural landscape under the Bakhtinian term of "polyphony". However, the central question of his chapter, it seems to me, is similar to the one posed by Gillespie and Zhuravkina: the Russian search for identity.

With the last chapter, written by Pernille Larsen, we cross the borders to post-Soviet Lithuania. In "Transition in Practice: Political Discourse and Market Patterns in Vilnius, Lithuania" Larsen publishes some of the results of the field studies she conducted in 1994-1995 on Gariunai, the largest wholesale market in the Baltic region. This ethnically mixed, 'transnational' and Russian speaking bazaar, Larsen shows, is perceived by society in general as a threat to the national political project of establishing a Westernised identity; consequently Gariunai, a product of 'the transition', is commonly considered a non-civilized and criminal space. As a carnivalistic chronotope or a 'cultural crossroad', places like Gariunai, Larsen maintains, 'challenge academic and political discourse on the transition by questioning the political project of a homogenous nation state, the creation of a Western-style market and the possibility of achieving a Western living standard'. Disagreeing with traditional views of the transition in the post-Soviet areas which tend to conjure up a Westernised future for Eastern Europe, Larsen instead suggests a vision of 'globalised Sovietism' with a tinge of "Asianism".

Thus we have returned to our point of departure, the problems of national unity, of mapping a nation's future and past. Often in this "mindscaping" of Eastern Europe, we rediscover the vast reservoirs of orientalism versus occidentalism, blended with the vestiges of old controversies between the Russian Slavophiles and the Westerners, and we are confronted with questions of self and other. Without falling into the traps of cynicism and nihilism, we should perhaps now be ready to accept not only the sameness but also the differences which we encounter in the post-Soviet societies of today.

The essays collected in this volume were originally prepared for the conference, "Soviet Civilization: New Interpretations?", which was organised by the Department of Slavonic Studies, Odense University, in December 1995. The conference was sponsored by grants from the research network, "Continuity and Change in Eastern Europe" under the Danish Research Council for the Humanities, and by grants from the Institute of Literature, Media and Culture and the Institute of History and Culture, Odense University.

The editors' thanks go to all the participants of the conference and to those who helped to organise it, and last but not least to Sally Laird who has thoroughly revised the English in the chapters written by the continental Europeans (any remaining linguistic error is, of course, the sole responsibility of the editors). Moreover, she has eminently translated the many difficult Russian citations in the contributions by N. Kozlova and I. Sandomirskaya.

Although the essays are written in British English, the editors have chosen the Library of Congress transliteration system in the bibliographical references and when Russian words are used in the texts. However, this convention is sometimes transgressed.

Reference

Haraway, D. (1989) *Primate Visions: Gender, Race, and Nature in the World of Modern Science*, Routledge, New York.

The Function of Lenin's Image in Soviet Mass Consciousness

OL'GA VELIKANOVA

During the decades of Communist rule, the myth of Lenin was a conspicuous feature of Soviet civilization, one aspect of the Soviet world outlook. The development of an ideal image of Lenin was an integral part of Communist party policy, the aim of which was to legitimise the Communist system and to mobilise the masses toward distinct goals. But it could not have succeeded if it had not corresponded to deep human needs, to pre-existing cultural values, and to political stereotypes upon which the Russian people relied.

This chapter will address the public representations and interpretations of Lenin's image in the 1920s and 1930s as well as in the 1970s and in the period of perestroika. Such an investigation of the Lenin "cult" inevitably requires attention also to the development of the cult of Stalin, with which it interacted. The main sources for studying this kind of political imagery, unavailable until quite recently, include new archive materials which document mass consciousness, including the political mood of the Soviet people. These new sources are the secret summaries of the Soviet political police and reports on "perlustrated" private letters (letters secretly opened by OGPU/NKVD). Additional evidence for this chapter includes uncensored folklore, museum collections, and sociological data.

Together, these sources demonstrate that Lenin's image in mass consciousness was not monolithic and simple but complicated and variable in its functions.

The image of Lenin existed in the collective mind of the people in several forms which responded to a variety of human needs, including the need for identity, the need for a protector, and the longing for integration. The image of Lenin served as a kinship symbol of "the father", as well as a religious, class, political, and national symbol with a variety of meanings. It even provided a model of behaviour.

The features of Lenin's image offered by the authorities, however, differed from the features generated in the imagination of the masses. In the masses' imagination of Lenin, one can distinguish various "hypostases" of his public image, such as Saint, Protector, and good Tsar, through which the religious tendencies of the people were realised. These were to a great degree spontaneous. In contrast, the more specific image of hero was inculcated from above and was offered as a model to be imitated. In the course of the evolution of this cult, the leader's image underwent several transformations. These changes in the image of Lenin corresponded with the developmental needs of a cult that existed throughout Soviet history and played a vital role. Of course, for 74 years Lenin was considered the embodiment of the Communist Party. But in the 1920s, he became the symbol of national integration; while in the 1960s, the humanising features given to his image represented an important contrast with the demonic image of Stalin, whom Khrushchev was vigorously discrediting. This chapter will focus on the different hypostases of Lenin's image among the masses.

The Irrational Dimension

Freud, Le Bon, Tarde and others transformed the intellectual study of politics and society by their recognition that "irrational" elements play a significant role in the maintenance of the social fabric and the social order. As this essay argues, the cult phenomenon cannot be understood only through a rational analysis of political theory and sociology. To study why a cult of the leader occurs, it is useful to draw on the methods of mass psychology and anthropology as well as to research the more specific and deeply-rooted beliefs, illusions and myths that made collective consciousness in the Soviet Union a kind of "secular religion", a social formation for which the irrational is a vital and perhaps unacknowledged component. According to George Mosse, a secular religion merely continues a phenomenon of primitive and Christian times in which a society views the world through myth and symbol, acting out the individual's hopes and fears within ceremonial and liturgical forms (Mosse 1975: 214). Emile Durkheim pointed out that even in the later stages of socio-cultural development, every society would require the "functional equivalent" of a religious system. Whether or not we call it "religion" is primarily a semantic issue. The point is that the mythological perception of the world can be realised not only in the form of historical religions but, in the process of secularisation, can adopt other forms. The socialist idea in the twentieth century can be understood as the secular embodiment of a religious system of representations.

As with other collective movements, appeals to the subconscious and the emotional existed in Russian Marxism. Led by Lunacharskii, Russian "God-builders" proclaimed that socialism needed to harness the inspiring force of myth to create a "religious atheism". The practical necessity of such a claim is not difficult to understand. By abolishing both the church and the monarchy, Soviet power had eliminated the primary cohesive forces in Russian society. The leaders could not avoid constructing a new system of beliefs that would explain the world and promote their goals. They needed secular religion to supply an alternative form of cohesion.

Marxism-Leninism in Russia developed into a theory which had all the strengths of a faith, so that one can in fact define it as a secular religion. The Communist counter-faith claimed that it possessed the ultimate truth about man and society which was declared once and forever in the scriptures of Marx and Lenin. There were new teachers to be believed in, ones who would show the way to a happy future and to salvation. A revealing, albeit critical treatment of this secular-religious outlook appears in a 1926 underground leaflet from the suburbs of Leningrad:

> The Communist Party, our sovereign, is hammering into everyone's head its point that this is the only right way to an earthly paradise, that this way has been shown by the "Genius" Lenin and

is now to be revered by the Party's instructions just as GOD and TSAR had to be revered previously... Citizens! Do you really need to have an object for divine worship, the way idols and icons used to be? Today it is Lenin's "immortal" spirit that bears the halo of worship.[1]

There is a considerable evidence that people perceived socialism as some kind of religion and the revolution as an act of creation. They saw themselves as the priesthood of a new revolutionary spirit. They found a new world worth living and dying for that gave them a feeling of being fully and entirely right, from which they derived a great stimulus and quasi-religious enthusiasm. For them, Marxism-Leninism contained many of the outward attributes of a faith with a system of ethics.

Erich Fromm considered faith to be a basic propensity of human beings. In his view, irrational faith is one's belief in a person, idea, or symbol that is not based upon one's direct personal experience, emotional or intellectual. Above all, it results in emotional subordination to some irrational authority (Fromm 1993: 154, 156). Hence, even in Stalin's camps, many prisoners refused to believe that Stalin had a hand in the terrible purges and incarcerations. They considered their own arrest to be a mistake, and they continued to believe blindly in the victory of Communism, all the time writing personal letters to Stalin assuring him of their love and loyalty. Among the key terms Stalinism invoked was "enthusiasm", which bears a close relationship to "faith", and "fanatical", the latter often being, in the Soviet context, a term free of negative connotation.

Psychologically, Fromm also asserts, a cult responds to man's tendency to give up the burdensome independence of his/her personality, to dissolve his/her ego in an outside force and thus to share in the power and glory he/she lacks as an individual: to become like a particle of a greater mass that is the leader, the Party, the nation, God, or a moral principle (Fromm 1990: 124, 135, 156). The deification of the leader and constant resurrection of his image are attributes of the cult that depend upon this type of irrational behaviour. A particular person, once transformed into a true God of the masses, becomes an infallible, legendary, and protecting spirit. Such deification is achieved by raising the per-

Lenin by N. Chekhonin. This picture was presented at the exhibition Revolutionary Russia in Petrograd, 1918.

son above the ordinary human level and placing him beyond all judgement. The person becomes a totally immaterial figure, immortal and perfect.

In spite of the state's policy of atheism, Lenin's image in Soviet Russia served as a religious symbol complete with such attributes as omnipresence, immortality and perfection.

Countless portraits as well as sculptures of him, all in public places, created an illusion of his omnipresence. The power of such visual imagery of Lenin should not be underestimated, especially in the pre-television era and in a country without a text culture, where the majority of the population was illiterate. As Jan Huizinga said, describing a phenomenon of the fifteenth century: 'Having once attributed a real existence to an idea, the mind wants to see it alive and can effect this only by personalising it' (Huizinga 1924: 186). In that distant past, 'the mere presence of a visible image of things holy sufficed to establish their truth' (Huizinga 1924: 165).

Such an analysis describes well the appeal of Soviet propaganda in the 1920 and 1930s. For example, the sense of the leader's omnipresence was reinforced by slogans imparting a similar message. In 1924, the response to Lenin's death unmistakably carries this sense: 'Lenin is silent now, but we workers can hear his voice inside us'.[2] Allusions to his omnipresence can likewise be found in characterisations of Lenin in Petrograd while he was still alive: 'Many of us have inherited, inconspicuously, at least a small particle of Comrade Lenin's works, of his tireless labour' (Zinov'ev 1918: 63).

The status of Lenin's image in a hierarchy of popular representations was marked visually in the interior of peasant homes. Beginning with the 1920s and during the Great Patriotic War, his portrait was often placed in the Icon Corner near the icons of the Russian Orthodox religion.

The significance of Lenin's image was also reflected lexically. The language of countless documents, both official and private, attests to the use of religious terms in reference to Lenin, thus indicating the 'dimension', or level, of public consciousness in which his image existed. In 1918 his close friend and comrade

Interior of a peasant home (*Prozhektor*, 1925, no. 2, p. 7).

Grigorii Zinov'ev named Lenin 'apostle of the Socialist revolution' and compared his book *What Is To Be Done* to the Gospel (Zinov'ev 1918: 8, 64, 27). In 1923, Trotskii wrote of Lenin: 'Marx was a prophet with tabernacles, and Lenin is the greatest executor of the testaments' (Trotskii 1991: 118).

Those who resisted the official system of values deployed a similar vocabulary, in which they struggled against Satanic forces of chaos; so that, whether in support of or opposition to it, the socialist revolution was imagined as a conflict between forces of order and evil analogous to those of religious systems. Lenin's opponents would often compare him to Satan or Anti-Christ (*Neizvestnaia Rossiia* 1994: 390-391). In private correspondence, people complained about Lenin in the following kind of language: 'People here have denied the true God and adopted, in place of God, Lenin-and-Trotskii the Satan, the bloodsucker, the cannibal'.[3] In the process of "de-Leninisation" that began at the end of the 1980s, the same tendency was discernible. Demanding the renaming of Leningrad at a meeting in 1990, citizens compared Lenin to the 'devil' in their slogans.

In the 1920s, following his death, Lenin was characteristically described as 'immortal'. Indeed, this was the primary motivation for the movement to preserve the corpse of the dead leader. Among party leaders the political interest of legitimising his successors was reflected in this tendency to present Lenin as 'immortal'. It was also a sign of their loyalty. But in the collective consciousness of the masses, the tendency to view Lenin as an 'immortal' figure belonged to a religious trend. Archives containing nine personal and collective letters from 1924 express in quasi-religious terms the authors' desire to preserve the body. In turn, the preservation of Lenin's embalmed body inspired the idea of his resurrection in the minds of the masses. This can be seen in rumours which circulated in the Ukraine around 1932, such as: 'Lenin has risen again and will come back soon to smash the Bolsheviks'.[3] During the mid-1920s, a legend circulated around Moscow that during the night Lenin climbed out of his coffin, walked out of the Mausoleum, and strolled around the Kremlin. This subject appeared in a similar form in a Viatka fairy tale from 1925. The story concerns the dead Lenin going to the Kremlin, to

Meeting in Leningrad on the Palace Square, 9 September 1990.

factories, and to the countryside, where he chatted with people along the way to find out how things were going without him. It ends as follows: 'In the Mausoleum, the deceased has lain down, satisfied… He will probably wake up soon. What happiness there will be then' (Piaskovskii 1930). In this story Lenin is a supreme judge, the single being who had the right to judge the correctness and truthfulness of the new socialist world. We can in fact see a similar idea of Lenin in the 1980s, when people, driven to despair by their lack of rights, would sometimes leave letters "to Il'ich" with their complaints on the barrier round his coffin in the Mausoleum, as if he was the ultimate source of justice.

The Father Figure

The iconography of the cult takes many different forms that respond to various human needs, but its foremost component is that of father figure. The cult worships the father of the church, the father of the nation, the father of the Party. Hence we recall that the Tsar was called 'Little Father' (*batiushka*) in Russia, and Stalin was called the beloved father of the Soviet people.

Societies with underdeveloped civil institutions and with unconstituted state systems often attempt to organise themselves according to an archaic type – to preserve a "family-type" organisation with the leader as father. The tendency to interpret the leader as father is strongest in traditional societies, especially under the institution of monarchy. But in the revolutionary society of Russia, the concept of a father-founder also had strong meaning. The new regime abolished any continuity with the past, but still needed its rituals and images of legitimation. The need for a father-founder, which plays a fundamental role in structuring society, was realised in the Lenin myth.

Immanuel Kant observed that the dependent relationship between a leader and the population often assumes the model of father and family and fosters suppression in society: 'A fatherly government, where subordinates, like adolescents, do not understand what is useful for them and what is not... such a form of rule is a great despotism' (translation from Russian) (Kant 1965). As if it consisted of nothing but family relationships, the whole governmental machine in such cases operates as a network of personal loyalties. Such a personal style of government had a tremendous appeal to a society which, after the sudden loss of the monarchy, still remained under the influence of dynastic feelings.

Indeed some peculiarities of Russian national character can be seen in the ordinary people's relationship to authority. According to one theory, Russian habits of obedience have been not the result, but the cause of political autocracy (Vakar 1961: 40). The autocrat was the image of autocracy which each child learned to accept in his or her family, which up to the beginning of the twentieth century continued to be patriarchal. Russian political culture, moreover, lacked any abstract notion of institutionalised power. The peasant was loyal to God rather than to the church, to the tsar rather than to the imperial government, to Lenin or Stalin rather than to the Party. A magnified "father cult", such as is found in all primitive agricultural societies, flourished in the cult of Lenin and, later, Stalin. It had grown so impressively large in the Soviet Union because the peasantry exerted such a powerful in-

Lithography *Il'ich* by V. Borovskii, 1970.

fluence on the development of collective representations in the 1920s and 1930s.

In the collective mind, Lenin filled this father role, responding to the natural human desire to have a protector who knows how

Drawing *Lenin with a Girl* by V. Zhukov, 1969.

to solve hard problems and who takes up the burden of responsibility. He promised to relieve them of the sufferings of war and to grant them land. He promised an imminent, bright future that was socialism. This side of Lenin's image was alive throughout the years of the cult. In 1924, for example, a female worker wrote: 'I came to believe in Il'ich. Now I understand why we mourn Comrade Lenin so deeply: it is because he is our guardian, the protector of all those oppressed'.[4] In the "mourning meetings" of 1924, the phrase 'we have become orphans' was very common. Later, in the 1960s, many *chastushki* (four-line folk rhymes) called Lenin 'daddy':

> Lenin, Daddy, wake up,
> And set Khrushchev straight,
> Vodka costs 27 roubles now,
> And there's no meat or butter at all.
>
> *(Lenin-batiushka, prosnis'*
> *I s Khrushchevym razberis'.*
> *Vodka stala 27,*
> *Miasa, masla net sovsem.)*
> (Kabronskii 1978: 189)

In this and many other *chastushki* Lenin plays the role not only of father but of supreme judge.

In numerous pictures of Lenin with children, the image of "daddy" or "grandad" appealed to the most basic human emotions.

Oktiabriata (the children of October) were called 'grandchildren of Il'ich'. In 1920, audiences of children were brought close to their leader in well-known events such as the New Year Tree Parties for children in Sokolniki or Gorki Park designed further to emphasise this paternal characteristic.

It was common in Bolshevik circles to call Lenin 'Il'ich', in an intimate, familial use of the patronymic alone. N. Valentinov wrote in his reminiscences: 'In his presence and in his absence he was called 'Il'ich'. It was common among comrades of the same age, but also among those who were older' (Valentinov 1953: 71). A certain familiarity is suggested by such naming, and it signifies an intimate relationship common to some closed community: a "com-

Poster *Oktiabriata* by N. Strunnikov, 1931.

munity" based on kinship or caste; or, more appropriately perhaps, the kinship of the Russian *obshchina* (peasant community). In the Soviet period, the nickname 'Il'ich' circulated not only in Party circles but among the public. A similar attitude, implying the sense of a large, patriarchal, peasant family, was evident in the naming of Stalin as 'Vissarionovich', or as *Khoziain* (Master), or oracularly as *Sam* (Himself). In this way, the transferring of the peasant houshold pattern of relations into power relations was reflected lexically.

Lenin Enters the Living Room

The fatherly image of Lenin allowed political culture to infiltrate private life, especially the household. Lenin's picture appeared regularly on everyday domestic and personal items. The Museum of Political History in St. Petersburg contains a platinum ring, a golden medallion, and shawls picturing Lenin and dated the

1920s. In 1924, 'Il'ich cigarettes' were available (with Lenin's silhouette on the pack), as well as Mausoleum-shaped inkpots and 'Build the Mausoleum' toys.

Cups and plates with the leader's portraits were ubiquitous in the 1920s. Later Lenin's pictures appeared mostly on decorative tableware and vases designed primarily for public display. This presence of Lenin's portraits in the everyday life of the 1920s, on items for practical use, suggests that his image was a "cherished" one which was kept in homes and carried on the body in the form of pendants and scarves. The perception of this phenomenon, however, gradually changed; thus a famous anecdote from 1970, concerning a three-person bed for newly-weds sold under the tradename 'Lenin Is Always With Us', suggests that Lenin's image had grown intrusive.

Sometimes this kinship symbol came into contradiction with the political symbol, as when Lenin the defender was seen as opposed to the Communist Party. In 1921 rumours spread in Petrograd that 'Lenin believed everything was in complete decay, and so he was surrounding himself with non-Communists and intended to hand the reins of government over to them'.[5] The image of a fatherly and caring Lenin was mostly spontaneous and developed among the common people. But at the same time it was used by the rulers to stimulate personal loyalty towards the leadership.

The Supreme Teacher

The father-image is closely connected with the image of Lenin as a supreme teacher, wise and omniscient: economics, literature, foreign affairs, and the secret of happiness were among the essential subjects of both private and public life about which Lenin was considered an authority. After Lenin's death, Krupskaia did much to inculcate this image into public consciousness through her numerous articles, such as: 'Lenin on Children's Nutrition', 'Lenin on the Study of Foreign Languages', 'Lenin on Communist Morals', and 'Lenin and the Working Woman'. But even when Lenin was only 24, his nickname among revolutionary circles was *Starik* – the old man. This was not simply a reference to his bald head. N. Valentinov, his colleague at the time, recalls: 'When Lenin was called *Starik*, this showed in fact a recognition of him as a *"starets"*, a wise elder and teacher in the spiritual sense of the word' (Valentinov 1953: 72).

This image of the wise teacher showed itself in photos and paintings portraying Lenin at his working desk, and in posters depicting him as the helmsman of a ship. In 1918 Zinov'ev called him the locomotive driver: 'Our locomotive is running breathtakingly fast. However, our driver is handling the locomotive perfectly. His sight is sharp, his hand is firm...' (Zinov'ev 1918: 61).

The image of Lenin as teacher is evident as well in the endless citations of his words in political and academic texts. In any given article, book or other piece of writing, to cite Lenin's opinion was to prove the legitimacy of the work, to mark its significance, and to emphasize the author's loyalty. These compulsory appeals to Lenin's works (and later to Stalin's) were dubbed 'Hallelujahs': repeated expressions of devotion to and glorification of the supreme authority. In the 1970s such references were parodied by the masses through jokes about a multi-volume publication called: 'The Classics (i.e. Lenin, Marx – O. V.) on Elephants'.

In this teacher-image, the rational element appears to be dominant. The teacher deserves respect because he has gained superior knowledge, because he has taught his pupils the "laws" of social development; because he has shown the way to salvation. The gesture of showing the way has been embodied in countless monuments, where the outstretched arm of Lenin leads its viewers toward some invisible, right direction to be discovered by attending to Lenin's teachings. In the 1970s there were several versions of the poster: 'Comrades, You Are Going the Right Way!'. These facets of the cult were developed with the greatest efficiency by Soviet propaganda.

Personifications

Most conspicuously, however, Lenin's image was used as a political symbol embodying the Communist Party, Soviet rule, and socialism. The portrait of Lenin became the symbol of the state, and from 1920 on was placed on the red banner next to that of Marx. The name of Lenin, personifying the Communist Party, was included in countless slogans. Vladimir Maiakovskii's rhyme: 'We say Party – meaning Lenin. We say Lenin – meaning Party' became one of many official slogans that provoked an eager response among the populace. The opinion that 'when Lenin dies, everything will go to pieces'[6] was very widespread, merely shifting tense after Lenin's death: 'There are rumours about an anticipated coup, as it is believed that the Republic cannot survive Lenin's death'.[7] This image of Lenin embodying the Party was constantly emphasised by the authorities and promoted, for example, in the 'Lenin Recruitment' to the Party in 1924. The identification of Lenin with Party and government was so close that his death caused doubts about the continued viability of the system (yet another reason why his immortality was important).

Hat Replaced by Cap

The perception of Lenin as the embodiment of the Communist Party was in its turn closely associated with his image as a class symbol. The proletariat was declared the bearer of Absolute Truth (i.e., socialism) while the bourgeoisie and the intelligentsia were denounced as parasitic classes. Of course, Lenin's image as leader of the World Proletariat, so carefully cultivated by the authorities, provoked the question of Lenin's own social origins. This was a touchy question in post-revolutionary Russia. Lenin's origins among the gentry did not fit at all in the official canon. For this reason Zinov'ev (perhaps consciously) misled the public when he wrote in 1918: 'Comrade Lenin's father was a peasant by origin' (Zinov'ev 1918: 8). The desire to create through propaganda an image of Lenin as class symbol gave rise to fabrications and omissions.

Lenin himself, however, was no less persistent in constructing his own image as the "people's leader". As soon as he came to power, his style of clothing changed dramatically. He discarded the hat, a piece of apparel which he had worn all his life, and which was typical for the bourgeoisie and intellectuals, replacing

Lenin's Arrival to Petrograd, 3 April 1917 by V. Sokolov, 1935.

it with a cap which became the most important detail of his clothing. In the last decades of the nineteenth and the first decade of the twentieth century, the cap became a universally-recognised sign of the working class in Europe (Hobsbawn 1983: 287). The last photo of Lenin in a hat was taken on his way from Stockholm to Russia in April 1917. He arrived at the Finland Railway Station in Petrograd wearing a dark hat too (Podvoiskii 1956: 115), but, in many memoirs of this event, Lenin appeared wearing a cap, and in fact all the iconography devoted to this event shows Lenin in a cap.

The identification of Lenin with a cap is so strong that a photograph discovered in the museum archives by the author, in which Lenin is shown on an armored car holding a black hat in his hand, has the following caption, dated 1930: 'From a picture of no artistic merit. The author is unknown'.[8]

The first photograph that gives evidence of the cap was used in forged documents when he wore the cap as a disguise while hiding in Razliv in July 1917. To be sure, we may assume that the cap had some idiosyncratic meaning for Lenin himself, perhaps as an indication that he was not a slave to fashion. In a detailed study of Lenin's last days, when he was seriously ill, N. Petrenko writes of Lenin's passionate attachment to his cap (Petrenko 1990: 286-287). He seemed never to part with it, even indoors. Evidently in his subconscious this piece of clothing had come to be of great personal importance to him. Nonetheless, this deliberate change of attire served also to emphasise his democratic approach, his accessibility, and his contact with the masses.

There were other episodes which also helped generate the image of Lenin as a class symbol. Since physical labour is an attribute of the proletariat, Lenin attended the *Subbotnik*, or Day of Voluntary Labour, on 1 May 1919, contributing by carrying logs. This act was captured by a photographer and got woven into the memoirs of several dozen people, all claiming to have carried a log together with the leader. Later the incident became the subject of various jokes.

The propaganda succeeded to such an extent that a worker who mourned him in 1924 declared: 'After the death of Il'ich, no one will defend the workers so staunchly and take care of their needs'.[9]

The Russian Lenin

It is normal for a leader to embody the dominant values and orientations of a society. Though the class idea had priority in the official Soviet system of values, emphasising an international vision of the proletariat, the reports of the political police unexpectedly show the significance of Lenin's image as a national symbol as well. In the first years after the revolution, when the idea of an international movement of the proletariat and the priority of class values over national ones was declared, this idea of Lenin as a national symbol was absent from the official propaganda. However, OGPU reports on public opinion show that the image of Lenin as an ethnic Russian, in the context of everyday anti-semitism, was of paramount significance for the masses. Summarising their findings, OGPU declared: 'Lenin enjoys the sympathies of the peasants because he is not Jewish'.[10] People considered this a decisive factor, sometimes ignoring the professional qualities of a political candidate as a result. For example, popular opinion about who should succeed Lenin after his death was epitomised by a statement from a worker, as reported by OGPU: '(Hope) Kalinin will be the next Chairman of the Government. He may be old, and lacking in willpower, but at least he's a true-blue Russian'.[11] It was probably this unanimous desire to see an ethnic Russian at the head of the government, and the prevailing nationalism, and anti-semitism registered by OGPU, which influenced the authorities' later policy of maintaining the ethnic purity of Lenin's image.

Successively in 1924, 1932, 1934, 1938, and 1965, the authorities refused permission to publish data on Lenin's Jewish or Kalmyk ancestors, a move suggested by A. I. Ul'ianova as a means of fighting widespread anti-semitism and by M. Shaginian in her novel *Ulianov's Family* (1958). Neither Stalin nor the Party leaders who came after him were willing to give up this aspect of Lenin's image, doing their best instead to keep their national symbol "immaculate".

But in the 1970s, despite the Party's efforts, rumours that Lenin might have had Jewish ancestry circulated among the public ('Note' 1994: 191). Such "suspicions" were reflected not only in KGB reports but also in uncensored folklore, including a number of jokes in which Lenin's speech patterns were called to attention:

What kind of Bolshevik is that
Climbing onto the armoured car?
He wears a cap
And can't pronounce his "r"s.

(Eto chto za bol'shevik
Lezet tam na bronevik?
Kepku on obychno nosit,
Bukvu "r" ne proiznosit.)

In the collective perception, failure to pronounce the 'r' was a characteristic not only of Lenin but of the speech patterns of Russian Jews; hence the slurred 'r' was perhaps associated in mass consciousness with Lenin's possible Jewishness.

This powerful nationalistic component in the mass perception of the leader is further reflected in cases where his image was adopted outside Russia. Thus Lenin's portrait was given anthropological features consistent with the Soviet republic or the Communist bloc country in which it appeared. Consciously or unconsciously, the artists thus brought this international class symbol closer to their own national focus, thereby easing acceptance of the image in their own nations. This process of transformation, in which Lenin's face subtly assumed the features of a Mongolian or Vietnamese, mirrored the process by which Lenin was transformed, according to the dominant social values, from a nobleman to a son of the peasantry.

Role Model

Yet another notable component of Lenin's image in the collective mind was his role as a hero, a model to be emulated. Although the qualities usually associated with the heroic image, such as physical strength, valour, and warlike deeds, were absent in Lenin's case, many monuments nevertheless presented his body as huge and muscular. Thus, for example, the monument by Anikushin, erected in 1970 in Moskovskii Prospekt, St. Petersburg, depicts a powerful, manly figure, which – if it were not for the overcoat – might well belong to a dancer or athlete.

As a figure for emulation, Lenin's image as a martyr who had suffered for the people became a central feature of Lenin portraiture, both after the attempt to assassinate him in August 1918, and after his death. This desire to emphasise his martyrdom may account for the unusually naturalistic details of the autopsy report. The grisly description of his brain condition, for instance, was reminiscent of the iconography of suffering saints, and implied the astonishing extent of his self-sacrifice to the people's cause.

Throughout all the phases of the Lenin cult, his image was consistently presented as one to emulate, most often as a moral example. This was explicitly recommended by Zinov'ev in his speech of September 6, 1918 to the Petrograd Soviet: 'Let us be at least a bit like Comrade Lenin' (Zinov'ev 1918: 64). The slogan of 1924, 'In Every Detail – Be Lenin!'[12] captures this intention even more succinctly. The Lenin model, moreover, was a commonplace in children's literature and in schoolbooks.

As a behavioural model, Lenin's image was remarkable for its uncanny ability to accumulate not only socialist dogma but features of Russian religious character. According to Russian Orthodox tradition, a major feature of holiness was austerity. Lenin's modesty and unpretentiousness in everyday life were always emphasised in the literature, and especially in the Lenin Museums and Memorial Homes. (Although in actual fact his homes and their furnishings were evidently more comfortable than the dwellings of common Soviet people: almost everybody was poorer than he and, unlike Lenin, lived in communal – i.e. shared for, hostel-type – apartments.) Still, Lenin's personal belongings, including his clothes, were exhibited in the Lenin Museum in Moscow to demonstrate his modesty. According to OGPU reports, the stories offered by propaganda, were interpreted by common people in quite specific ways: '26.01.1924. Shipyard. A worker said, "It's biting cold, but they won't hand out any gloves to us". Those standing by rushed to reproach him, saying he should be ashamed: 'Take Il'ich, he worked barehanded, and never asked for gloves'".[13] The legends of the leader's simplicity often caused the museum visitors to ask, 'How did Lenin manage to survive?'. Austerity thereby became the sign of Lenin's faithful service to the people.

The behavioural model carried by Lenin's image also included sexual asceticism. The image of the leader depends in certain respects on traditions of sexual behaviour in the given culture. In Russian Orthodox culture sex is considered a sin. It was not among the central values in Soviet culture, as was reflected in a common phrase: 'There is no sex in the USSR', first pronounced out loud by a participant in a TV discussion during the perestroika period. The asexual image of Lenin embodied the virtues of the Soviet ethic. Although Lenin was married, Krupskaia's image was entirely devoid of sexual attributes. According to myth, she was no more than a comrade and fellow-in-arms. A very typical question among children, who were convinced that Lenin loved them immensely, was: 'Why didn't Lenin have children?'. Museum workers routinely answered this by saying that Lenin was very busy with his revolutionary activities. When the children grew up, this idea was transformed in their subconscious into a belief in the leader's sexual immaculacy. In Memorial Homes the beds of Lenin and Krupskaia always stood separately, even in Shushenskoe where they got married. Family life was excluded from the official image of all the succeeding Soviet leaders, whose wives were absent from official rituals. Their absence was not only a tribute to the influence of the East, which focuses attention on the man, but also a sign of the leader's devoted service to the people.

All these facets of Lenin's image, closely interrelated and sometimes, mutually contradictory, co-existed in his cult. At different periods, one or other side of that image acquired greater importance and prevailed over the others; but together they responded to and capitalised upon basic needs inherent in Russian culture (if not in human nature).

Deconstruction of a Myth

From the 1980s onwards, each facet of Lenin's image was gradually eroded in the minds of the masses. The political symbol of Lenin, as the embodiment of a happy socialist future, was the first to collapse. A new ideal, capitalism, replaced it, and the old symbol could find no place in the new system of values. That symbol has vanished together with the socialist state itself. Everything has changed. Flags, medals, and coins that once assured Lenin's continuing presence no longer carry his image.

Lenin as symbol of the wise teacher has been undermined in articles by Seliunin, Kliamkin, and Tsipko, who have subjected his "teaching" and policy to thorough criticism. The kinship symbol has also been shattered. The miraculous protector and defender whom Lenin was supposed to personify failed to live up to expectations which were illusory from the very beginning (Fromm 1990: 149-152). Indeed no one could ever live up to such fabulous expectations, and disappointment was inevitable. 'The miraculous defender' has been turned into a scapegoat of contemporary disappointments. Lenin has been declared responsible for all the country's misfortunes in the twentieth century.

As a national symbol, the image of Lenin has been destroyed in the most perfidious way. The rumours that Lenin was a Jew circulated among philistines in the 1970s and 1980s, and archive documents on the national origin of Lenin's ancestors, published in Russia in 1992, substantiated these claims. And in the 1990s, as in 1917, the story of money received by Lenin from the German government for revolutionary activities hurt people's national and patriotic pride. Since Lenin played the role of superior moral authority, the disclosure of his actual moral behaviour has been a severe shock to people's feelings. The image of a kind and understanding leader was smashed once newly-published documents proved him guilty of merciless terror, of approving the firing-squad execution of priests, and of instituting the food collection policy which led to mass famine.

This image of a cruel politician has been supplemented by evidence of Lenin's personal cruelty. A letter written by Krupskaia artlessly tells of an episode during a hunt, in which Lenin mercilessly killed a number of hares that were crowded on a tiny island, trying to escape a flood. This story was especially painful since every Russian cherishes from his or her childhood the story of Nekrasov's *Uncle Mazai*, who rescued hares from the flood in his boat.

Likewise, his modesty in everyday life has at least been brought under suspicion. A study of the Ul'ianov family correspondence has yielded the information that Lenin during his exile to Shushenskoe had a servant, ordered himself a hunting gun from Belgium, and procured a pack of hunting dogs, all these suggesting conditions of some luxury, especially when compared to the conditions of exile in Soviet times.

The legend of Lenin's sexual chastity has completely withered away. A book and private letters have been published, documenting the relations between Lenin and Inessa Armand, a pretty aristocrat. Journalists have drawn public attention to the abusive language used by Lenin in his works, including words such as 'fool', 'idiot', 'hysteric', 'crazy', and 'blockhead', which appeared in philosophical and political discussions. Thus Lenin's image as a moral model has also been destroyed.

The Inertia of Collective Consciousness

Every reason to deify Lenin seems to have vanished. Yet data from public opinion polls show that about half of those queried still regard Lenin as a positive symbol.

Although polls provide a superficial idea of public opinion, it is nevertheless evident that a vast number of people, especially those belonging to the older generation and living in the provinces, avoid negative information on Lenin and have not changed their positive attitude toward him. How can this be explained? First, changes in collective consciousness occur slowly. Moreover, it is psychologically understandable that people might seek to avoid the discomfort caused by any information that contradicts established stereotypes. Many people have objected to the methods of "de-Leninisation", such as the desecration of monuments or the intrusion into private lives which they consider to be a form of "muckracking". The view 'that you shouldn't hurt a man who can't answer back' is very common. What can this mean? The traditional pity of Russians for the defeated, or simply the view that *de mortuis nil nisi bonum?*

There is perhaps another explanation. The image of Lenin which cemented political religion existed in a "faith dimension" rather than in a rational one. Rational arguments have prevailed in the destruction of the image, but they do not operate in the "faith dimension". No deeply held religious faith is open to rational dialogue. Although the unifying symbol has been shattered, there is nothing around to replace it. No charismatic personality exists in today's political environment upon whom people can rely, in whom they can embody their hopes, or whom they can invest with the aura of miraculous protector. According to the latest sociological data, over 70% of those polled consider that Russia yet again needs a strong leader, believing that he or she alone can bring order to the country (*Argumenty i fakty*, no. 4, 1996).

Notes

TsGAIPD SP Tsentral'nyi Gosudarstvennyi Arkhiv Istoriko-Politicheskikh Dokumentov Sankt-Peterburga.
RTsKhIDNI Rossiiskyi Tsentr Khraneniia i Izucheniia Dokumentov Noveishei Istorii.
GM PIR SP Gosudarstvennyi Muzei Politicheskoi Istorii Rossii v Sankt-Peterburge.

1. TsGAIPD SP, f.16, op.1, d.61,ll.38-39
2. TsGAIPD SP, f.16, op.9, d.9765, l.17
3. March 1924, TsGAIPD SP, f.16, op.5, d.5911, l.102
4. RTsKhIDNI, f.124, op.3, d.359, l.26
5. RTsKhIDNI, f.16, op.1, d.528, l.149
6. TsGAIPD SP, f.16, op.5, d.4319, l.32
7. TsGAIPD SP, f.16, op.5, d.5335, l.66
8. Ibid., l.25
9. GM PIR SP, f. 4 vs, N 3141/1
10. TsGAIPD SP, f.16, op.5, d.5335, l.55
11. RTsKhIDNI, f.16, op.1, d.98, l.10
12. TsGAIPD SP, f.16, op.5, d.5335, l.64
13. RTsKhIDNI, f.16, op.1, d.49, l.59

References

Dal', V. (1880) *Tolkovyi slovar' zhivogo russkogo iazyka*, Moscow-Petersburg.
Fromm, E. (1990) *Begstvo ot svobody*, Progress, Moscow.
Fromm, E. (1993) *Psichoanaliz i etika*, Nauka, Moscow.
Hobsbawn, E. (1983) 'Mass-Producing Traditions: Europe, 1870-1914', in E. Hobsbawn and T. Ranger, eds, *The Invention of Tradition*, Cambridge University Press.
Huizinga, J. (1924) *The Waning of the Middle Ages*, London.

Kabronskii, V., ed. (1978) *Nepodtsenzurnaia Russkaia Chastushka*, New York.
Kant, I. (1965) *Sochineniia* v 6 t., Moscow.
Mosse, G. L. (1975) *The Nationalization of the Masses. Political Symbolism and Mass Movements in Germany from the Napoleonic Wars through the Third Reich*, Howard Fertig, New York.
'Note of KGB to TsK KPSS on Students Moods, 5 November 1968', in *Istoricheskii Arkhiv*, no. 1, 1994.
Petrenko, N. (1990) 'Lenin v Gorkakh – Bolezn' i Smert' (Istochnikovedcheskie Zametki)', in *Minuvshee. Istoricheskii Al'manakh* 2, Atheneus, Moscow.
Piaskovskii, A. V. (1930) *Lenin v russkoi narodnoi skazke i vostochnoi legende*, Molodaia gvardiia, Moscow.
Podvoiskii, N. I. (1956) 'V. I. Lenin v 1917', *Istoricheskii Arkhiv*, no. 6.
Neizvestnaia Rossiia: XX vek. Arkhivy. Pis'ma. Memuary, no. 4, 1994, Istoricheskoe nasledie, Moscow.
Trotskii, L. (1991) 'O ranenom' in A. Lunacharskii, K. Radek, L. Trotskii *Siluety. Politicheskie portrety*, Progress, Moscow.
Vakar, N. (1961) *The Taproot of Soviet Society*, Harper and Brothers, New York.
Valentinov, N. (1953) *Vstrechi s Leninym*, Izdatel'stvo imeni Chekhova, New York.
Zinov'ev, G. (1918) *Lenin*, Petrograd.

Proletarian Tourism: Incorporated History and Incorporated Rhetoric

IRINA SANDOMIRSKAYA

In a recent public opinion poll among Western politicians and intellectuals, the USSR won the majority vote for the nomination of "the country of the century". The historical project called "the Soviet Union", the most colossal of all the projects of Modernity, has obviously come to an end. However, Soviet society, as a product of Modern cultural history, is far from being extinct. As an object of study, moreover, it has been attracting growing interest worldwide, and the more attention it receives, the more of a challenge it presents to Western theoretical models. There have been attempts to extend post-modern theories to cover Russian discourse, but thus far this has led to an obfuscation of these models rather than an elucidation of the situation. Besides, Russian discourse is generally felt to resist attempts at "translation" into a common European model. Clearly, "the Russian soul" is determined to claim one of the top positions in the list of research subjects for the coming 21st century.

The greatest problem with social research on 20th century Russia is the nature of Soviet textual sources. No one believes them any more. Often, newly-discovered documents are so bewildering in their absurdity, so strikingly inexplicable, so full of passion and vindictiveness, so disarmingly naive that they immediately provoke doubts as to their very authenticity. To question the veracity of a given text, however, is a forbidden move in the intellectual game called post-modern philosophy.

The research suggested in this chapter is not exactly cultural history. Rather, I would call it a "history of Soviet rhetoric". I suggest an approach to the discourse of the Soviet period as idioms of Russian culture.[1] The obvious advantage of this approach is that an idiom is a sign that has no truth-value but is the smallest discursive formation of the lexicon and a building block for a rhetorical device.[2] Thus, expanding the notion of the idiom to extra-verbal contexts such as Stalinist tourism would not, at least, endanger the graceful theoretical constructions of post-modern social theory, whose negligence towards truth-value is a strong theoretical advantage (cf., for instance, the "cult" of truth-value and the resulting methodological restrictions in analytical philosophy).

As a linguist by profession, I also suspect that the so-called "linguistic turn" in the social sciences has actually been a U-turn. The linguistic turn in historical research, for instance, has been brought about by the application of Saussurean dichotomies as refracted through the lens of semiotics. However, Saussurean linguistics is only one theory of symbols among others, and as a system of interpretation its limitations are only too evident now.[3]

It is important to remember that the Saussurean linguistic system was never intended for the explication of idiomaticity and cross-cultural differentiation.[4] The obsession with Saussureanism among social researchers is the factor which prevents the linguistic U-turn in the social sciences from completing another U-turn, thus achieving a 360 degree turnabout, a complete revolution.

Another source of inspiration has been found in Walter Benjamin's theory of translation.[5] Following Benjamin, I understand translatability (in the broadest possible sense) as a property of semiosis which provides for the general capability of One (culture, historical community, ethnos, class, group, individual, etc.) to understand Another (culture, historical community, ethnos, class, group, individual, etc.). When viewed from this angle, idiomaticity would be the only factor of semiosis to produce misunderstanding. Exotic historical forms of discourse, such as that of Stalinism, could thus be discussed in a panchronistic aspect, in which questions of veracity or authenticity would become irrelevant.

Proletarian Tourism

A forgotten phenomenon of early Stalinist society, proletarian tourism (PT) is a fascinating subject for research.[6] In terms of symbols and figures of everyday life this episode of Soviet cultural history can give us insight into the nature of symbolic power at large.

Tourism (both in its European version as a form of pleasure-seeking and in its Stalinist version as a form of revolutionary Crusade) appears to be motivated by a common metaphor, also found in world mythologies: Life is a journey/Death is the end of a journey. Sacral connotations of 'the Way' pervade European cultural myths, from folk tales to Christian dogma (Toporov 1994). My assumption is that 'the Way' as a sacred symbol is what elevates recreational practice into an object for the investment of personal desires. It would be interesting to examine how individual desires are related to collective cultural connotations, how cultural identities evolve through interaction with such connotations, how physical human bodies are transformed into living symbols of cult and tradition and how a social institution eventually develops into a cultural idiom.

The main source for the following study are the texts included in a pre-war journal published by the Society of Proletarian Tourism and Excursions *(Obshchestvo proletarskogo turizma i ekskursii)*, a publication called *Na sushe i na more (On Land and Sea)*. The publication was terminated in 1941 after OPTE, the Society of Proletarian Tourism and Excursions, was disbanded, its patron, (the People's Commissar of Justice Nikolai Krylenko) shot and several members of the editorial board arrested.

Genres of Revolutionary Recreation

In terms of demographic processes, PT (proletarian tourism) can be described as a form of recreation. However, judging from my sources, it was recreation of a very unusual kind.

Below is an account of a 'military-cultural excursion' published in one of the earliest issues of the journal, *Na sushe i na more*.

> Account of a military-cultural excursion undertaken by students at the Lenin Educational Community in Kabardino-Balkaria.
> Students reported on their work to 12,000 listeners in 18 settlements. In these settlements over 25,000 Karbardino-Balkarian work-

ers were involved in various aspects of their cultural work. Over 7,000 people attended discussions, lectures and speeches.

In addition, graduating students and teachers conducted a number of investigations and undertook the instruction of local organisations: Komsomol cells, Pioneer organisations, schools, soviets and cooperatives; the dissemination of books in the national language was also studied. A subscription campaign to the newspaper *Karakhalk*, undertaken by the students, resulted in 500 new subscribers, none of whom had previously subscribed to any newspaper.

With regard to practical work, the students gave 26 talks involving 2,440 persons; some 98 newspaper readings involving 1,230 persons, 8 newspapers readings by Pioneers involving 90 persons; and 9 talks with [political] maps involving 400 persons. Regarding the work of the OSOAVIAKHIM (The Union of Societies of Friends for the Defence of the Aviation and Chemical Industries – I.S.), some 10 talks were conducted involving 560 people, and 11 Pioneer discussions involving 490 people. Seven KSM (i.e. Communist League of Youth – I.S.) cells were investigated, along with 9 cooperatives and 2 wall newspapers. Some 120 books were sold by Pioneers, along with 805 pictures and posters, and 1,560 books of literature were distributed in village reading rooms. A political raffle was conducted involving 1,550 people; 48 presents were handed out; 8 campaign wall newspapers were issued by students, and 2 by Pioneers. 35 local contributions were included. All newspapers were left in the settlement.

4 plays involving 900 people were put on in local languages, 14 film shows involving 6,000 people took place; there were 5 physical culture performances involving 2,500 people; 492 people were enlisted to subscribe to the local newspaper *Karakhalk*. One cell of the ODN (the organisation "Down with illiteracy" – I.S.), including 14 members, was organised, as well a cell of the OSOAVIAKHIM, including 22 members. Donations to MOPR (the international Organisation to Assist Revolutionary Fighters – I.S.), totalling 82 roubles, were collected, and MOPR literature was sold for 3 roubles. In addition, several of the poorest households and land workers were investigated (*Na sushe i na more*, 1929).[7]

Another very peculiar genre of proletarian tourism took the form of the *kraevedenie* (regional study trip). While the aim of the military-cultural excursions was a revolutionary transformation of social reality (such as the godforsaken village in Kabardino-Balkaria mentioned in the illustration above), such educational expeditions were directed towards the revolutionary transformation of the tourist himself, namely, the acquisition of a new vision, new knowledge, new skills – and, to top it off, a new corporeality. Below is an extract from a tourist account of one such educational journey:

> It is only now, in recollection, that we have been able sufficiently to appreciate the value of our boat trip on Lake Vyg (a lake in Karelia – I. S.).
> The boat journey afforded us great educational material which was exceptionally valuable in being of a graphic nature. Visiting plants and factories, we followed the course of several forms of production, and were able with our own eyes to see the success of Soviet technology and the growth of the country's industrial might.
> Various aspects of the life and work of the state – transport, industry, trade and foreign relations – were presented before our eyes.
> We experienced in ourselves the health-giving influence of the journey. In the course of one's everyday work one pays little attention to the life of one's own organism. The journey gave us heaps of fresh air, sunshine, and energetic and varied exercise. We learned to swim, to row, to steer the vessel in all weathers. Overcoming obstacles, we acquired habits which will serve us throughout our lives. In addition, before the journey several of us had at times sensed in ourselves a certain apathy, a "couldn't care less" attitude. The journey renewed us: we came into contact with genuine life (*Na sushe i na more*, no. 6, 1929, p. 16).

As well as serving the purposes of ideological propaganda and enlightenment, tourism can be observed to have played another important role, that of transforming political violence into a carnival, the horror of famine and repression into a feast of collective enthusiasm. The following is a further article from *Na sushe i na more*, an account of a *massovka* (recreational/ideological tourist attraction for the masses):

> Agricultural Technology Campaign in the Chapaev District Proceeds Successfully.
> In preparation for the XVII Party Congress the Middle Volga Soviet of the OPTE (the Society of Proletarian Tourism and Excur-

sions – I.S.) organised an agricultural technology campaign in the Chapaev District. The intention, according to the plan, was for the excursions to involve an exchange of experience with 500 kolkhoz workers through as many one-day visits to kolkhozes and villages, and to arrange for 1,000 persons to make excursions to the city.

By 20 January 409 persons had taken part in the Agrotechnology campaign. The main object of the excursions were the sovkhozes and communes covered by the Bezenchukskaia Motor-and-Tractor-Station, where the kolkhoz workers were acquainted with the achievements in socialist agrotechnology and the results of work in the first year of the second five-year plan.

In the Komintern kolkhoz excursions were conducted on the theme "The results of the economic year in the kolkhoz"; in the Commune "The Flame of Revolution", on the theme "Agricultural work in the Commune and new indicators of work in its branches". In the Chapaev pig sovkhoz the following themes for excursions were put forward: "The sovkhoz as a centre for livestock rearing" and "The care of pigs" [...]

As a result of these excursions the kolkhoz workers made a number of valuable suggestions.

In "The Road to Communism" kolkhoz, named after the Tula workers, and "The Route to Victory" kolkhoz, the following proposals were accepted: a method of giving out fodder according to need, rather than leaving it in a heap; the steaming of fodder in tubs; the rational distribution of snow fences; the need to acquire a minimum knowledge of agrotechnology and elementary mechanisation, and certain constructive changes in harvesting. In the Komintern kolkhoz of the Nikolsky village it was decided to adopt model methods for the preparation of spring sowing (distribution of work forces, timely repairs of agricultural equipment; the organisation of fodder stores and so on).

The Dzerzhinsky kolkhoz passed on to other kolkhozes its experience in constructing a communal bath house, using a copper boiler made from scrap metal, and in using the remains of horse fodder for the common herd of cows [...]

Besides the kolkhoz workers, workers of sovkhozes and the Motor-Tractor-Station as well as children took part in the agrotechnology campaign. Schoolchildren from the Chapaev pig sovkhoz organised a campaign under the slogan "Parents, join the ranks of the shock workers of the XVII Party Congress" (*Na sushe i na more*, no. 4, 1934, p. 4).

Thus, three genres of tourism as a form of discursive practice can be identified, all of them characterised by a specific type of rhetoric.

The first sample, the military-cultural excursion, largely relies on the rhetoric of figures. Statistical data (possibly veracious) are used in this type of rhetoric for the political legitimation of recreation: political activity during a collective outing thus appears both useful for the regime and healthy for the body. Ideological correctness is shown to be an inseparable part of the body's well-being.

In the second quotation, the discourse of the body is related to the pleasures of boating plus the satisfaction of observing the recent progress of Soviet economics and technology. The interesting point here is that the newly-acquired knowledge (concerning technological processes) and skills (swimming, sailing, etc.) both have the effect of physical revival, and, significantly, a revival of desire. A lesson in the economic geography of the USSR turns out to be a lesson in "genuine life".

Finally, in the third quotation, the traditional ideology of the peasant community (neighbours helping neighbours in agricultural activities) is re-interpreted in the blatant rhetoric of collectivism, a concept that claimed priority in the new consciousness of the reformed (dekulakised, collectivised) peasantry. This piece of carnivalised (and still authentic) ideological writing reads like Andrei Platonov. However, it should be remembered that we are not dealing with a text of fiction. We are dealing here with a cultural idiom of carnivalised early Soviet social reality.

A Cultural Idiom as a Product of Translation (1): PT vs Russian Pre-Revolutionary Tourism

While a non-idiomatic word has (semantic) structure, an idiom can be said to have an infrastructure, i.e., an internal logic of symbolic communication that provides for exchange between meaningful components within the structure of a symbol.

In terms of infrastructure, PT can easily be seen to have derived its basic components and the inner logic of a cultural construction from its pre-revolutionary predecessor.

In Geineke (1932) we find a history of tourism and excursions in Russia in which attention is drawn to the difference between these two forms of social activity (an excursion is a method of education, tourism is a social movement).

According to Geineke, Russia's first tourist organisation was *Krymskii gornyi klub* (1890) (the Crimean Mountaineering Club) with its monthly publication, *Zapiski krymskogo gornogo kluba*. The aims of the club were: the study of the Crimea, assistance to tourists travelling in the Crimea, support for local agriculture, gardening and small businesses, and the preservation of nature and cultural values.

In 1902, the first mountain climbers' organisations were established: the *Kavkazskoe gornoe obshchestvo* and *Kavkazskii gornyi klub*.

The *Rossiiskoe obshchestvo turistov* (Russian Society of Tourists) (ROT, 1895) was an organisation that promoted tourism as a sports activity, arranging bicycle races and so forth.

Russian educational tourism was a system with a well-developed infrastructure. Prior to 1914 certain basic principles of tourism were established, such as: the development and management of tourist routes and of tourist bases equipped for lectures, seminars and laboratory studies; the organisation of local excursions from these bases, the setting up of travel discounts and the publication of tourist guides.

As early as 1918-19, in the wake of the October revolution, research and activities connected with the organisation of excursions were resumed. In 1923, the Central Institute of Museums and Excursions *(Tsentral'nyi muzeino-ekskursionnyi institut)* resumed long-distance educational excursions to the Crimea. In 1926, the *Sovetskii turist* joint stock company was founded. In 1927, ROT was transformed into a mass proletarian organisation. In 1930, *Sovetskii turist* was merged with ROT to form the OPTE. This was the starting point for the history of PT.

Judging by what we can (or rather, cannot) read in *Na sushe i na more*, OPTE was somewhat jealous of its pre-revolutionary prototype: not a single mention of it can be found. This is a significant omission, for OPTE claimed the status of a "social invention", whereas in fact its practical agenda seems to have been copied from pre-revolutionary tourism.

Why such "jealousy"? The reason becomes clear if one considers the ideological message carried by OPTE:

> [...] to infuse all the methods and forms of its work with the interests and tasks of strengthening the defence capacity of the country [...] to develop the ability to move in difficult conditions, the ability to orienteer on location and in natural conditions, to temper and develop character, sharpness of vision, courage, endurance and other qualities necessary to the future fighter in the Red Army (Krylenko and Gurvich 1933).

In a speech to a plenary meeting of the Central Board in 1933, Krylenko called on OPTE 'to look at their work as a method of socialist construction'. Political activities were proclaimed the principal purpose of the union.

Despite comparable "infrastructures", OPTE and pre-revolutionary Russian tourist societies were not identical discursive formations but mutually opposed cultural institutions with distinct idioms. The difference was purely ideological: OPTE's agenda was that of proletarian revolution, where ROT's was obviously not. This is why articles in *Na sushe i na more* never refer to pre-revolutionary forms of tourism as the predecessors of their own. On the contrary, "proletarian" tourism is presented as a crusade for the holy mission of World Revolution. PT vehemently condemns Western commercial tourism as 'bourgeois' and 'an instrument of imperialist propaganda'.

A Cultural Idiom as a Product of Translation (2): PT vs Forms of Organised Leisure Among German Proletarians

In a Granat entry on the German working class (Glaubauf 1931), one can easily identify another cultural idiom that must have served as an ideologically correct source for PT to have been translated from. The encyclopaedia contains interesting data about tourism among post-war German proletarians.

In the section on forms of organisation of leisure, Glaubauf notes a difference between pre- and post-war generations of German workers: the former would spend their leisure time drinking, while the latter were more interested in collective recreation and activities, including the gardeners' movement, people's theatres, workers' singing clubs and sports. "Friends of nature" *(Die Naturfreunde)* was reportedly one of the most popular movements, a successful combination of education and recreation.

Social-democratic "leisure management" structures also took care of post-war migration and unemployment problems. For instance, the "Migrant Bird" *(Der Wandervogel)* movement was organised by trade unions to facilitate workers' migration in search of new jobs. The movement was strongly supported, in terms of legitimation, by reference to the old tradition of German guilds who would send apprentices out on journeys on foot around the country before they could be admitted to professional corporations as full members.

German communists were very active in these organisations, but the social-democratic and liberal message, judging by the article in Granat, was much more successful.

Thus, PT's own definition of tourism as 'one of the stages along which the masses perform their ascent towards the heights of culture' *(Na sushe i na more,* no. 3, 1929, p. 10) does not seem very innovative when compared to its German counterpart .

Another (and most significant) similarity can be found in the strategy of communist propaganda. Glaubauf openly declares seduction to be the most advantageous method employed by the ideological machine run by the German Communist Party:

> It is not accidental that functionaries of the proletarian organisations in Germany are called "confidential agents": the method of their work, which even now is widely used in the Communist Party, consists in winning the confidence of Party and Union comrades by infiltrating their private lives.

The communist strategy of "constituency management" was therefore aimed at the worker's (or, in fact, voter's) personal life, and the cultural and social capital thus won was, as the article explicitly states, confidence.

A similar orientation towards seduction through the gaining of confidence is evident in OPTE. Though official documents endowed proletarian tourism only with the functions of agitation and conviction, its strength too lay in the power of seduction. The intention to seduce (and win confidence) permeated the speeches made by those appointed to enlighten the masses on the subject of tourism. It was evident in the speaker's manner and behaviour, his good looks, his image as a young, conscious (*soznatel'nyi*), healthy, happy, self-assured and incredibly up-to-date *Angelus Novus* of the world revolution. Seduction was openly formulated as a task of a tourist: 'The pride of the tourists is at the disposal of the masses, whom they win over to the Party and to Soviet power' (*Na sushe i na more*, no. 1, 1930, pp. 1-2).

What made OPTE's agenda strikingly different from the German communist programme of "constituency management" is the concrete (and explicitly stated) purpose of such seduction. 'Winning over the affection of the masses' was declared as the primary objective of PT as an instrument of the Party and the State: PT's main aim was 'the fulfilment of the socio-political, military and economic tasks of the Party and the State' (Antonov-Saratovskii 1930). This is evidently the reason why in OPTE's publications there is practically no mention of the "German colleagues", apart from a couple of short notes that produce a rather ambiguous impression.

Considering that both PT and German "social-democratic" tourism shared a common position with respect to the body (steel muscles, etc.), it would be interesting to compare PT's military/athletic programmes with the corresponding programmes of the German Communist Party. However, I have no material as to the role of the German workers' tourist organisations in the preparations for the 2nd World War. Nevertheless, data obtained from *Na sushe i na more* indicate that it was in the context of "readiness for war" that the discourse of the body was "plugged into" the general discourse of PT, as was, indeed, the motif of seduction.

Conclusion

As I have tried to show, PT was a very special Stalinist "innovation" that appears absurd at first glance but in fact manifests an inherent, if invisible logic, the logic of an ingenious civilising device.

At the same time, what gives proletarian tourism a pre-eminent position among other civilizational devices of Modernity is its unrestrained readiness for violence. Its military ambitions were not only a sign of the time, but also, I think, a symptom of the Russian soul – an interesting subject that has to be omitted from this discussion.

Above, I have given an outline of proletarian tourism as an ideological machine and as an institution. My main interest has been in proletarian tourism as an idiom of early Stalinist culture, a transposed signifier of a cultural connotation.

The agenda of this institution becomes more understandable when we take into consideration the indirect (transposed, idiomatic) significance of proletarian tourism as practice. The mechanisms which drove this institution forward were not only political interests, but also the repressed desires of individuals. I would generalise this individual motivation as a desire for signification, i.e., the irresistible thrill of being signified by an authoritative symbol and the still more irresistible thrill of exerting one's own power in the act of signifying the world.

One can see that the desire of individual (self)-signification gives tremendous support to a political institution, especially if the latter claims absolute dominance over the symbolic sphere. Moreover, a political claim would merely be a derived product of desire, since any institution is, ultimately, a group of individuals with individual life projects.

Desire is not subject to state violence: what is suppressed cannot be repressed. However, suppression can act as a force of political manipulation. Reciprocity of intentions (contrary to the unidirectional intention of repression) is the key concept for understanding independent *(samodeiatel'nye)* institutions of power such as proletarian tourism. An approach to such oxymoronic *(samodeiatel'nost'* and power) formations in terms of cultural idioms shows that everyday social reality has two important dimensions: that of incorporated history (a historical project) and that of incorporated connotation (a rhetorical project).

Notes

1. I have been inspired by the example of Jacques Derrida (Derrida 1993) who proposed looking at Stalinism as a historical idiom.
2. See Sebeok 1986 for a historical outline of the philosophic and linguistic argument between logic and rhetoric, truth and metaphor, etc.
3. For a critique of Saussurean sign theory see, for instance, Derrida 1976.
4. Recent research in linguistics confirms that idiomaticity and associated pragmatics should be viewed as the starting point of linguistic theory, especially with a view to cross-cultural communication. One might refer to the works of Halliday 1979, Fillmore and co-workers (e.g., 1988), Wierzbicka 1991, Teliya and co-workers 1991, Nunberg 1994 and many others.
5. 'Languages are not strangers to one another, but are, a priori and apart from all historical relationships, interrelated in what they want to express' (Benjamin 1978: 72).
6. Encyclopaedic data on proletarian tourism are scarce (e.g., 'Turizm' in *Bol'shaia Sovetskaia Entsiklopediia*, v. 26, p. 132). According to this encyclopaedia, proletarian tourism (the All-Union Voluntary Society of Proletarian Tourism and Excursions, OPTE, see below) was instituted by a decree of the Council of People's Commissars in 1930 on the basis of a joint-stock company *Sovetskii turist* (1928). In 1930, it had 169,000 members and in 1932, 937,000. It also had 92 tourist bases of All-Union status. A total of 6, 6 m. people took part in long-distance and local journeys. In 1936, OPTE was transformed into TEU *(Turistsko-ekskursionnoe upravlenie)* under the auspices of VTsSPS *(Vsesoiuznyi Tsentral'nyj Sovet Professional'nykh Soiuzov)*. According to *Bol'shaia Sovetskaia Entsiklopediia* and other encyclopaedic sources, OPTE's head N. V. Krylenko (1885-1938) was a member of the first Council of People's Commissars and after March 1918 was responsible for the institution and organisation of the Soviet court and procuracy. Prior to 1931, he was a public prosecutor at major political trials; from 1922 until 1931 he was Chairman of the Supreme Martial Court and Deputy People's Commissar of Justice, and assistant to the Procurator of the RSFSR. After 1936, Krylenko became People's Commissar of Justice. From 1928 to 1934 Krylenko headed OPTE, and during this time he organised and led a research expedition to the Pamir. After 1929, he became head of the USSR Chess and Checkers Section and between 1925 and 1936 initiated a series of international chess tournaments. In 1938, Krylenko was relieved of his high-ranking position, dismissed, arrested and shot as an enemy of the people.
7. Unfortunately, I cannot give a more precise reference, since I failed to note the number of the relevant issue when I first read it. When I ad-

dressed the Lenin library fund for additional information, I failed to identify the issue in which I had found the quotation.

References

Antonov-Saratovskii, V. (1930) 'Turizm, partiia i gosudarstvo', *Na sushe i na more*, no. 1, pp. 1-2.
Benjamin, W. (1978) 'The Task of the Translator', in H. Arendt, ed., *Illuminations*, Schoken Books, New York.
Derrida, J. (1976) *Of Grammatology*, The Johns Hopkins Univ. Press, Baltimore and London,
Derrida, J. (1993) *Filosofiia i literatura // Jacques Derrida v Moskve: dekonstruktsiia puteshestviia*, Moscow.
Fillmore, Ch., P. Kay, M. C. O'Connor (1988) 'Regularity and Idiomaticity in Grammatical Constructions: the Case of Let Alone', *Language*, vol. 64, no. 3, pp. 501-538.
Geineke, N. (1932) 'Ekskursionnoe delo i turizm', *Entsiklopedicheskii slovar' russkogo bibliograficheskogo instituta Granat*, 7th edition, vol. 51, pp. 450-458.
Glaubauf, I. (1931) 'Rabochii klass Germanii', *Entsiklopedicheskii slovar' russkogo bibliograficheskogo instituta Granat*, 7th edition, vol. 34, col. 741-747.
Halliday, M. (1979) *Language as a Social Semiotic. The Social Interpretation of Language and Meaning*, Edward Arnold, London.
Krylenko, N. & L. Gurvich (1933) *Boevye zadachi; Vyshe kachestvo turistskoi raboty*, Ts[entralnii] S[ovet] OPTE, Moscow.
Nunberg, G., I. Sag, T. Wasow (1994) 'Idioms', *Language*, vol. 70, no. 3, pp. 491-538.
Sebeok, T., ed. (1986) 'Rhetorics', in *Encyclopaedic Dictionary of Semiotics*, Mouton de Greuter, Berlin, New York, Amsterdam.
Teliya, V., ed. (1991) *Chelovecheskii faktor v iazyke: Iazykovye mekhanizmy ekspressivnosti*, Nauka, Moscow.
Toporov, V. N. (1994) 'Put'', in *Mify narodov mira. Entsiklopediia*, vol. 2, Moscow, pp. 352-353.
Wierzbicka, A. (1991) *Cross-Cultural Pragmatics. The Semantics of Human Interaction*, Mouton de Gruyter, Berlin, New York.

This research was made possible by financial support from the Open Society Institute (OSI/RSS 1994-1996).

The Days of Dogs and Dolphins: Aesopian Metaphors of Soviet Science

METTE BRYLD

Animals often function as substitutes for humans. When the fruit fly became *persona non grata* in the Soviet Union around 1950, it was not because of any damage caused by the tiny insect itself, but because the poor fly was transformed by the regime into an icon of human wickedness and perversion. Being the preferred experimental animal of the geneticists, ousted for their rejection of the official doctrines on the inheritance of acquired characteristics, the fruit fly was deprived of its significance as an insect in its own right and became, instead, the very symbol of rotten, bourgeois thought. The story of the fly, whose name, *Drosophila*, was for a period surrounded by powerful ideological taboos, is, of course, just one example of how animals may serve as mirrors of ourselves or of our (human) enemies. Cultural history, encompassing the natural sciences, abounds in such mirror reflections of animals as humans, and vice versa.

To some critics of Soviet society, Stalin's reinvention of the human and I. Pavlov's reinvention of the animal were two sides of the same coin. In his book, *The Soviet Political Mind* (1963), the historian Robert C. Tucker claims that the tyrant in the postwar period did intend to transform his subjects into Pavlov's passive, salivating and harnessed dogs by implementing the technique developed by the physiologist of learning through conditioned reflexes. Tucker thus argues that the despiritualised model of personality, forced on Soviet psychology by the party around 1950, was based on the simplistic notion 'that there is nothing in man that transcends in principle the conditioned salivary responses of Pavlov's dog' (Tucker 1963: 108). In other words, Stalinist society and the Pavlovian laboratory were in Tucker's eyes more or less identical. Similar views have recently been promoted by post-Soviet scientists who for obvious reasons have been eager to disown the past. To the nestor of the Russian physiological sciences, professor I. A. Arshavskii, for instance, the alliance between Pavlovian experiments and the Party's reconstruction of society was founded on a shared mechanistic outlook which perceived animals as well as humans as mere machines. In need of human cogs, Soviet power supported Pavlov's transformations of the dogs into animal cogs (*Nezavisimaia Gazeta*, 13 September 1994).

Both the above-mentioned scholars thus envisage Soviet civilization as entangled in a web of circulating meanings, where dogs are turned into machines and where, on the other hand, these beast-machines are displaced to, and even fused with, humanity in the formation of what might be called a doggy society. Half animal, half machine, the dog-cog becomes the mirror reflection of debased *Homo Sovieticus*. This staging of Stalinist civilization as a Pavlovian laboratory suggests a number of horror stories: above all, perhaps, the scenario in which the master of science, whether Pavlov or Stalin, is seen engaged in experimenting on his mute and tortured puppets with the aim of transforming the whole of society and living nature in accordance with his own goals. Furthermore, a comparison between the laboratory and the new society, which only enforces such gloomy connotations, was naively made even by Pavlov himself when, in a speech at a Kremlin reception in 1935, he likened his own work to the government's. 'As you know', Pavlov said, 'I am an experimenter from top to toe. All my life has consisted in experiments. Our government is also an experimenter, only of an incomparably higher category'. Amid stormy applause the ageing scientist then proposed a toast to 'the great social experimenters' (Pavlov 1951: 20).

In this chapter, I shall take up the Aesopian metaphor embedded in these discourses, all of which in one way or another use the animal to expose a human condition. I shall first examine the Stalinist elevation of Pavlov's physiological animal studies which may, indeed, be interpreted as an attempted doggification of the population, at any rate on the symbolic level.[1] Second, I shall look into the question of what happened within the Pavlovian school of biology with this equation of man and animal during the period of de-stalinization, when the quest for a non-biologised and renewed humanity was placed on the social agenda. While, as we shall see, a neo-Pavlovian fraction of scientists in the post-Stalin period tried to discard the Aesopian angle altogether in order to celebrate Man, liberated of degrading brutishness, outright anti-Pavlovians in the 1960s set up, on the contrary, an Aesopian counter-image of their own. In the strange and alien shape of the wild dolphin, young biologists thus put forward a grandiose vision of another society, based on the then popular notion of a socialism with a 'human face'.

As the Aesopian frame of this chapter may suggest, a significant underlying theme in the mirroring of man and animal displays the unsettled, nomadic quality of Soviet discourse on what a human being is. Despite seeming ideological uniformity, various, deeply contradictory possibilities were opened up. Is man really nothing but a Pavlovian dog, a pitiful beast-machine? Or is he, on the contrary, the proud human being in control of the world, signified by Man with a capital M, – that is, the peak of evolution, as anthropocentric materialism pathetically claims? Or, finally, should man rather acknowledge his many and fatal shortcomings and, instead, strive to be something else – a gently smiling Dolphin, perhaps?

The Alliance Between the Party and Pavlov: The Making of a Beast-Machine

In order to illustrate the question of the animal, mirroring man, I shall outline, as briefly as possible, the rise of Pavlovian science in the Soviet Union and the obvious fascinations it held for the Communist Party.

Although Pavlov was openly hostile toward the Bolshevik regime, the Party quickly indicated an interest in keeping the old Academician (b. 1849) from leaving the country. In 1921 Lenin issued a decree stating that a special committee, with prominent members such as Maksim Gor'kii on its board, should be set up to create the most favourable conditions for safeguarding the work of Pavlov. The decree baited the trap by significantly improving the living conditions of his household and, perhaps more importanly to the conceited scientist, holding out the prospect of publishing a de luxe edition of his writings. Special funding was furthermore assigned to the Academy's physiological laboratory, headed by Pavlov, enabling its gradual expansion. Around 1930, a large biological station, popularly known as 'the capital of conditioned reflexes', was built for his experiments in a village near Leningrad, and a few years later the newspapers reported that the government was raising Pavlov's Institute to all-Union status, 'designating it the centre for the "all-round study of Man", the Magnitostroi or Dneprostroi of the medical sciences' (Joravsky 1989: 328).

The importance ascribed from above to the Pavlovian doctrines on man and animal was once more underlined in 1934, when the Academy's Presidium changed the name of Pavlov's Institute to the Institute of the Physiology and Pathology of Higher Nervous Activities, thereby stating what physiology was all about. By this renaming the Academy of Sciences had also officially sanctioned, in its only physiological institution, the policy of keeping its research exclusively within the extremely reductionistic frame of Pavlovian thought (Lange 1975: 34).

However, it was only in 1935, after Pavlov had finally declared his full allegiance to Soviet power that he was hailed as a truly Soviet scientist. Up until then, the problem of separating the one Pavlov, who flatly rejected Marxism and the legitimacy of Bolshevism, from the other Pavlov, who had initiated 'progressive' and 'revolutionary' scientific teachings, had been solved by hinting at his advanced age and declaring him simply incapable of overcoming his conservatism in social questions. After the fusion of the two Pavlovs into one single visionary Soviet figure, the last obstacle to a genuine Pavlov worship was removed. From now on any criticism, however cautious, from fellow scientists who regarded Pavlovism as too mechanistic was severely rebuked by the guardians of Stalinist ideology; the materialism in which the dog studies were rooted, was, they claimed, by no means mechanistic, but purely dialectical (Joravsky 1983: 590).

Though initiated long before the revolution, Pavlov's science was, as I have indicated, extremely attractive to the new regime. I shall mention four reasons for this. First, Pavlovism was entirely materialistic, based as it was on studies of purely physiological processes. All notions of mind, soul or psyche were totally expelled from the scientist's allegedly strictly objective vocabulary. Instead, Pavlov had coined the expression, 'higher nervous activity', to designate what in ordinary language is commonly known as mental. Such a re-definition suited the new authorities well and 'higher nervous activity' became the established Soviet name for everything connected with brain functions. In 1931, the so-called small encyclopaedia illustrated the point by bluntly stating that 'higher nervous activity' was the proper term for what was earlier called the 'soul'. The Pavlovian paradigm, developed almost exclusively on studies of dogs, thus offered a strong scientific weapon in the Party's battle against religion. Typically, it was also this antireligious and anti-mystical aspect of the natural sciences which was stressed by Molotov in the speech he delivered to the participants at the International Congress of Physiologists hosted by the Soviet Union in 1935. 'Contemporary physiology, which is materialistic in its very foundations', said Molotov, 'contributes, together with the development of other sciences, to the liberation of man's intellectual evolution, emancipating him from all this mould of mysticism and religious relics' (*Pravda*, 18 August 1935).

As a demonstration of the new symbiosis between official ideology and his own doctrines, Pavlov presided over the Congress which – grateful, perhaps, that the old man did not drop dead during the demanding proceedings – bestowed on him the honorary title of 'the elder of the world's physiologists' (*stareishina fiziologov mira*). I shall later return to the significance of this title, which was afterwards referred to with great pride in almost all Soviet writings on Pavlov and in my view played a certain role in his glorification.

Second, Pavlovian materialism was so simplistic that it was easily subsumed under Stalin's clumsy definitions of the hierarchic relations between the outer, material and the inner, psychic world. These thoughts, originally put forward in Stalin's work, *Anarchism or Socialism* (1906), were incessantly quoted during the party's promotion of Lysenkoism and Pavlovism in the late 1940s and early 1950s. At the Pavlov Session jointly convoked by the Academy of Sciences and the Academy of Medical Sciences in 1950, S. I. Vavilov in his opening speech referred, as might be expected, to Stalin's doctrine that the development of external conditions preceded the development of consciousness, using this to confirm the greatness of Pavlov.[2] The creature envisaged by both Stalin and Pavlov was entirely in the grip of the social or the scientific experimenter.

Pavlov's teachings on conditioned reflexes undoubtly attracted the Party because they situated the organism, human or animal, in a pseudo-interaction with the environment which perfectly suited the official philosophy. In 1931, the above-mentioned encyclopaedia promoted this view by indicating that the higher nervous activities represented only a series of answers, or reflexes, by which the nervous system responded to stimuli from the outside. 'Man's life is built on reflexes', the encyclopaedia asserted, making it clear that once the law of reflexes was fully known, science would comprehend the behavioural mechanisms of both humans and animals. (A similar point was at the same time made by A. Afinogenov's popular play *Fear (Strakh)* which depicted Soviet society in the shape of a Pavlovian laboratory.) Thus, already at this early stage, Stalinist culture envisaged the control of behaviour through the implemention of Pavlovian scientific methodology. So highly evaluated was Pavlovian science that, from Stalin's time until the collapse of the Party, it was even glorified as the scientific, and hence final, proof of Lenin's doctrine of consciousness, his so-called theory of reflection. By this bizarre device, characteristic of the unsettled, nomadic discourse of Soviet ideology, the poor, passive animal object of Pavlov's experiments and the proud, wilful, extremely active man of Lenin's theory of the mind were thus made identical.[3] As we shall see, this identification was, indeed, true to Pavlovian dogma, which did not really differentiate between human and animal; on the other hand, however, it did not quite match the picture of elevated Man embedded in Lenin's acclaimed theory.

Third, in the 1930s, when the foundation of the Pavlov cult was being laid, the concepts of workshop, factory and laboratory started to fuse and become synonymous. Science was to get out of the universities and institutes into everyday working life and, vice versa, laboratories were to function as factories; phrases such as 'the physiology of labour' and 'factory and workshop laboratories' became part of the new language.

Pavlov's laboratory fitted well into these trends, since for many years already it had been staged as a factory with the famous mongrel dogs serving more as mechanical machines than living creatures. Bound by ropes or fixed in a harness, the Pavlovian dog, trained in advance to accept passivity, was unable to move. Furthermore, its body was surgically submitted to reconstructions so that the biological functions investigated were laid visually bare; the stomach, for instance, was separated in two with the second, small stomach serving as a 'window' into the larger, digesting one; or parts of the dog's brain were removed so that the scientists could study the behavioural disabilities caused by this operation. During the chronic experiment,[4] the harnessed animal was isolated in what was the world's first completely controlled environment, a sound-proof room, a *camera silenta*, where it could be observed and manipulated by the scientist, who was situated outside (see the illustration). From his voyeuristic position, the scientist could also measure the dog's output: the amount of saliva, for example, that the animal produced in response to the stimuli provided by the experimenter. The reconstruction of the body involved various wires, drains and so on, which were placed both inside and outside the animal.

At the start of an experiment, the scientist would typically give the dog a signal by ringing a bell, flashing a light or giving the dog an electric shock before feeding it. Eventually, the animal would learn to connect the signal with food in a conditioned reflex; the signal became, in other words, a substitute for food. The proof of the developed reflex would be that, at the given signal, the dog produced saliva or gastric juice, indicating thereby that it associated the signal with food. Through a drain the secretion was delivered to the scientist as the output of the beast-machine; this secretory output was thus the prime signifier of the whole process. The fact that the entire doctrine of higher nervous activity was founded on studies of salivary functions in mongrels

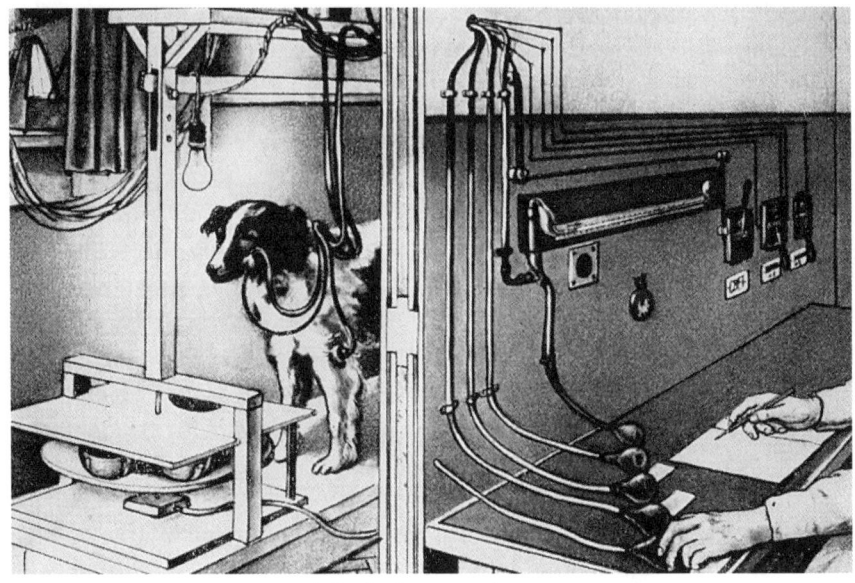

A Pavlovian experiment.

could evidently only strengthen the metaphorical bonding between the Pavlovian laboratory and the new society, preoccupied as it was with the hunger of the lower classes.

One section of Pavlov's laboratory was moreover called 'the gastric-juice factory'. As a result of the scientist's innovative surgery, gastric juice would be collected from a number of dogs on whom a special operation on the gullet had been performed so that the food which they took into their mouth and swallowed would fall out of the gullet into a dish before it reached the stomach. But the stomach reacted as if it was being fed, and hence generated gastric juice in large quantities for the laboratory. The sham feeding would normally go on for several hours with the dogs naturally getting hungrier and hungrier. One of Pavlov's enthusiastic biographers and former assistants, Babkin, claims that 'large, hungry dogs could produce 1,000 cc. of gastric juice at one session' (Babkin 1971: 131). Up to twenty litres of the juice were at one time collected daily. Uncontaminated with saliva or food, the dog-juice, pure as water, would then be sold as medicine to

The Days of Dogs and Dolphins

pharmacies and doctors who prescribed it to patients with digestive problems. Babkin notes that the remedy never became popular as a medicine, 'due to the inconvenience of its administration'. Even though twice diluted with water, he says, it still had an 'unpleasantly sour taste. The juice had to be taken in large quantities, being sucked through a glass tube so that its acid would not damage the teeth' (Babkin 1971: 70). Nevertheless, the sale of gastric dog juice provided Pavlov's laboratory with a steady income, and other sources, eager to emphasize the practical implications of Pavlov's innovation, insist, on the contrary, on the success of this medicine in both the Soviet Union and abroad (see, for example, Bykov 1948: 11). To Pavlov, digestion was, in beast as well as in man, a 'chemical factory'. His gastric juice section, with the dogs serving as 'inexhaustible factories', was therefore a quite logical realisation of this view.

The fourth and final reason for the Party's interest in Pavlovian science takes us back to the question of Pavlov's honorary title of 'elder', a title which may be related to the new and symbolic importance of the natural sciences as levers for establishing an ideology of paternalistic materialism in a society allegedly under scientific re-construction. As already noted, in 1935 the International Congress bestowed on the by then eighty-five-year-old Pavlov the title of 'elder', thereby placing him in the significant

The principle of sham feeding as shown in Pavlov's *Collected Works*.

context of an ongoing "grandfatherification" – a trend which counterbalanced the period's strong emphasis on youth and the radiant future by giving weight to secular origins and intellectually fertile roots. A new societal genealogy was emerging, involving the notion of old, yet wise and creative father-figures.[5] M. Kalinin, titular head of state since 1923, was commonly known as 'grandfather' and 'all-Union elder'. With his white beard and genial smile he fitted the role perfectly. So too did Pavlov, though in a much more serene and austere way.[6]

The grandfatherification of Soviet civilization was undoubtedly connected also to the substitution, in popular cultural iconography, of members of the political and scientific community for erstwhile God or priest. Created in the image of a fatherly god, an orthodox priest must, then as now, be fully bearded – as Pavlov was. Thus the ideologically important replacement of idealism with materialism was quite graphically demonstrated by Pavlov, as well as by other of the period's grandfather-scientists.[7] However, the man with the dog had a quality which perhaps made

Pavlov in the 1931 encyclopeadia.

him extra-well-suited to serve as special icon for the Darwinian theory of evolution, by now the only politically admissable theory of the origin of man. He had, especially in his old age, a certain likeness to both Darwin and the ape. The resemblance is more evident in some pictures than in others, but it is nevertheless suggestive. This icon, fusing Pavlov with Darwin, not only hinted at the animal ancestor, visually and metaphorically present in one of the founding fathers of modern materialistic science. It also suggested the overcoming of the animal past. Darwin was the celebrated genius of science, and Pavlov, the first Russian Nobel Laureate, was a neurophysiologist, a brain specialist, famous for studying the brain's signals to the mouth and the stomach, traditional regions of dumb animal matter. Like Darwin, Pavlov too represented matter's glorious jump from stomach to brain, – that is, from beastly unconsciousness to human self-consciousness. Embracing, on the one hand, the animal mirror of man, the ambivalent discourse of Stalinism endorsed, on the other, the pathetic image of Man. An ambivalence already suggested by the double image of the Pavlovian dog reflecting Lenin's proud human being.

The Dog Days and the Unmaking of Animal Man

The ambivalence was nevertheless only barely audible in the Pavlov Session of 1950, which was convoked with the intention of terrorizing scientists into becoming true Pavlovians. For it was extremely difficult at one and the same time to be a true Pavlovian and to reflect the image of the proud man since the mentor educator himself had not basically differentiated between animal and human. As the 1931 encyclopaedia had correctly stated, in its presentation of Pavlov's views, man's life was built on reflexes, just like a dog's.

A few years before his death in 1936, Pavlov had, however, rather casually formulated a distinction between the human and the animal. While an animal, the scientist maintained, had only inborn and conditioned reflexes, all of which belonged to the so-called 'first signal system', man possessed, in addition to this first system, a 'second signal system' which, to a certain degree, distinguished him from the dumb beast. This second signal system consisted in the ability to speak and think in abstract and symbolic terms. But even if speech, according to Pavlov, was precisely what made us human, our nervous activity, including neuroses and psychoses, could still be examined by analyzing the brain functions and reflexes of higher animals such as dogs. In Pavlov's own words, 'the fundamental laws governing the activity of the first signal system must also govern that of the second, because it, too, is activity of the same nervous tissue'.[8] The difference between the two kinds of beast-machines was due solely to levels of complexity. Having a much more complex brain than the animal, man was a much more highly-developed beast-machine, an extraordinary or even 'social animal', as Marx once said. Though nothing but a cliché disguised as science, Pavlov's distinction was later, during the time of de-stalinization, slightly revised and re-used by his followers who, by separating the human from the animal, hoped to shelter the otherwise homeless concept of Man with a capital M.

But the 1950 Session was still much too terrorized to embark on any revisions of Pavlovian physiology, which had been elevated to the status of dialectical materialism. One telling example of the few, rather vague attempts to separate man from animal, was provided by one of the main speakers at the Session, professor A. Ivanov-Smolenskii. Referring to the development of language, the second signal system, as determined by history,[9] he argued that the first signal system, the inborn and conditioned reflexes, similarly evolved within society, and that it would therefore be wrong 'in man's first cortical system only to see the biological part of his higher nervous activity' (Nauchnaia 1950: 101). But this almost self-contradictory point was never elaborated, and the same went for the sporadic warnings against mechanistically applying the results of animal research on humans.

Caught in an ideological double bind between, on the one hand, signals from Stalin's decree that man was a social creature, determined by history and external conditions, and, on the other, by signals from the great Pavlov, telling them that the 'fundamental laws', governing the work of both the first and the second signal systems, originated in the 'same nervous tissue' – that is, in biology – the scientists were in much the same situation as the harnessed Pavlovian dogs.

Not surprisingly, the crumbling of crude Pavlovian indoctrination within Soviet science during the Thaw, was accompanied by a condemnation of Stalin's 'tendency, associated with vulgar-materialist views, to biologize man' (Tucker 1963: 118). Thus the attempt to re-humanize society after the tyrant's death went hand in hand with efforts to de-animalize man in the various sciences that had been influenced by Pavlov's mechanistic outlook, such as psychology, neurophysiology, physiology, biology and medicine. Finally, in 1962, Pavlovism was more or less officially dismantled as a dogma. But this does not mean that the doctrines of the great mentor, or his loyal disciples, simply disappeared from the scientific scenario. Pavlov's works were still being published, as were uncritical, admiring books and articles about him. He was still regarded as a truly Soviet scientist, the counterpart to the philosophical Lenin, as well as a great Russian 'patriot'. Moreover, his teachings, including of course his mechanistic terminology, were maintained and (mis)used in the ensuing decades by his scientific followers, often as indisputable evidence and, hence, final proof of nothing less than the (re-)discovered great divide between speaking Man and dumb animal. The fundamental (physiological) laws, mentioned earlier, were no longer said to govern the life of humans.

Thus, in 1977, a prominent physiologist and ardent neo-Pavlovian, L. G. Voronin (b. 1908), painstakingly summed up the by now well-established notion that language, man's so-called second signal system, not only differentiates him from the animal, but actually invalidates his brutishness, since it makes his biological bonds to animal matter invisible. Voronin explained his new understanding of the transformation of animal man into what he called a 'social being' (not a social animal) as follows:

> Pavlov separated man's higher nervous activity into the first and the second signal systems. He took for granted that the signal system of animals and the first signal system of man were identical in their mechanisms and laws of activity. However, the difference

generated by man's becoming a social being makes possible the claim that his signal systems are inseparable from each other. The second signal system dialectically "invalidates" and transforms in itself the characteristics of the animal: that is, it masks the general features of the biological bond between man and animal. By virtue of this, it is incorrect to speak of any rudiments of a second signal system in animals (Voronin 1977: 103).

In this revised and slightly modernized version of Pavlov, speaking Man became unique and superior, while the animal continued its mute existence as a purely mechanical beast-machine, deprived of all psychic categories.

Pavlov had viewed man (and beast) as wholly determined by the mechanical law of reflexes; his followers subsequently liberated the human from this iron grip by transforming him into a social being, whose superior place in the world was based on the inferiority of the dumb animal. But in spite of such efforts to restore Man, the neo-Pavlovian revision of the old doctrines could not make a clear break with the fundamental ambivalence of the Stalinist discourse, promoting both the picture of Lenin's proud, wilful human and of Pavlov's mindless dog. The one still did not move without the other.

Socialism with a Dolphin Face:
An Aesopian Metaphor of the Counterculture

During the 1960s, however, a strange new animal challenged the established iconography. Introduced by anti-Pavlovian trends within the biological sciences, this creature conjured up an Aesopian metaphor of its own, one which reflected the alternative, gentler society that many humans longed for at the time.

This dissident creature, whose image replaced both that of the mindless beast-machine and Superior Man, was the dolphin. In 1966, an article in *Izvestiia* presented dolphins as 'our true sea brothers' and stressed the mammal's very large and complex brain, so 'strikingly close to our own'. Painted in nuances that were easily recognisable as communist virtues, the newspaper's dolphin turned out to be an ideal, peace-loving and helpful comrade with very high morals: 'Characteristic of the dolphins is a feeling of comradeship; they are unselfish in their relations to each other and always rush to help at the first call, even at the risk of their own death' (*Izvestiia*, 13 March 1966).

The article moreover reported scientific expectations of imminent communication with the sea mammals, first in dolphinese and later probably in Russian. In response to the creation of this astonishing animal, an official ban was at the same time announced on the catching and killing of dolphins for anything other than scientific purposes.

The humanised dolphin originated in the West. Reconstructed by an American neurophysiologist, John C. Lilly, the speaking and ethically-minded dolphin swam into the public Soviet pool shortly after the dismantling of dogmatic Pavlovism. At the end of 1962, the largest popular scientific magazine in the Soviet Union, *Nauka i zhizn'*, boldly published an article by Lilly, bearing the quite startling and provocative title, 'How I Learned to Speak with My Dolphins'. Here it was disclosed that Lilly had not just spoken with his dolphins in the way people usually communicate with their cat or dog. Eager to establish contact, the brainy animals, it transpired, had more or less answered him in English. In 1965, Lilly's book, *Man and Dolphin* (1961), which advocated similar ideas, was translated into Russian. A few years later, L. G. Voronin, forgetting the by now, perhaps, somewhat embarassing dogs, could claim that, apart from the monkey, no animal had caught the scientists' attention as had the dolphin, and especially the bottlenose dolphin, the one which smiles (Voronin 1970: 191).

Following the introduction of the talking dolphin, the mysteriously smiling marine mammal became the battleground on which, for some two decades,[10] neo- and anti-Pavlovists fought a cautious, yet unmistakable war on the intriguing question: who is really the most human, proud man or the gentle dolphin? This seemingly scientific controversy was thus in itself a kind of Aesopian debate on the very issue of what Soviet civilization is or should strive to be.

On the one side, the neo-Pavlovian establishment claimed the indisputable superiority of Man, citing his ability to speak and think in abstract and symbolic terms (that is, his possession of a second signal system). Pavlov, as one neo-Pavlovian asserted, had after all maintained that language was the privilege only of the large and complex human brain. Therefore the dolphin brain, no matter how enormous, could not be compared to the human, nor could a speaking dolphin exist in contradiction of Pavlov's law (Tomilin 1965: 87). The animal's huge brain, the scientist went on, was just the result of its adaptation to the special environment of the sea; absolutely nothing in the mammal's behaviour indicated anything beyond the usual instinctual gestures of a beast-machine. Lacking speech, human brains and, hence, technology, this mammal – like, indeed, all other animals – was solely in the grip of blind, mechanical instincts. Insisting on the inferiority of the dolphin brain in all respects, another neo-Pavlovian dismissed the whole issue as a storm in the teacup of popular science. 'What should the dolphin really think with?', this scientist rhetorically asked, making the huge marine mammal brain vanish as an illusion (Kesarev 1968 and 1971). Faithful to the basic doctrines of their old mentor, these life scientists still pictured the animals through his severe eyes. The animal was no more than a machine designed to serve scientific Man. (Cf., for instance, the title of Tomilin's book, *Dolphins Serve Man* (1969); see also Tomilin 1980; L. G. Voronin 1970; E. N. Panov 1980.)

On the other side, a few, mostly younger biologists, to whom the Pavlovian paradigm was obviously both dangerous and outmoded, insisted on the superiority not of Man, but of the Dolphin. In their view, man, and perhaps especially Soviet man, was implicitly the one who lacked all the dolphin virtues: collectivity, non-aggressiveness, culture, wisdom, memory of the past as well as harmony with the environment. The most persistent dolphin fan among the scientists was the then very young Aleksei V. Yablokov (b. 1933)[11] who many years later, in 1989, became president of the national Greenpeace organization as well as deputy chairman of the committee of the Supreme Soviet on ecology. Subsequently he was appointed chief advisor to President Yeltsyn on environmental issues.

An important mission of the 'intellectuals of the sea', as the anti-Pavlovians more than once called the dolphins, was obviously to lay out a new, alternative Aesopian metaphor of Soviet civilization; to advocate, in other words, a dolphin state rather than a doggy state.

Among the striking features of the kind, peaceful dolphin society described by Yablokov and his colleagues, V. Bel'kovich and S. Kleinenberg, in their popular science books of the mid- and late sixties, were the astonishing cultural, emotional and ethical bonds which kept the animal community together. Even more striking, perhaps, was the scientists' claim that this bonding was due to nothing less than a "grandmotherification" of dolphin society. The foundation of this community, the authors claimed, was the family, tied together by strong emotions, and always headed by the mother alone. Reaching sexual maturity very early, a female dolphin could give birth to as many as ten young during her lifetime. This reproduction pattern would inevitably result in the rapid grandmotherification of the dolphin herd, since the female off-spring would reproduce just as quickly too. The outcome would be a large, extended family of at least eleven generations of simultaneous daughters-mothers-grandmothers, with the oldest and so to speak primordial (grand-grand-etc.) mother at the top (see the illustration).

According to the anti-Pavlovians, this grandmammyfication created a marvelous dolphin culture since 'the living memory of the ancestors' was always present. The collective memory of the dolphins was compared with an enormous library, reinforcing the image of the animals as naturally talented intellectuals who stored up the traditional wisdom of oral literature and legends in their huge brains.[12] For even if they allegedly possessed the equivalent of libraries, the sea mammals had, of course, no books, no technology, nothing of the technological culture which man, the scientists stated, had been forced to invent in order to compensate for his imperfect, underdeveloped organism. So, in the displaced view of these scientists, the dolphin might well feel superior to man. 'Humans', their matriarch dolphin regretfully sighed, 'do not understand the meaning of life. They try with raw force to subjugate nature' (Bel'kovich 1967: 325). In contrast, the dolphins themselves had it all in their bodily nature and in their mind. As superior beings they were endowed not only with a fantastic me-

A civilization of caring grandmothers (Bel'kovich 1967: 317).

mory, but with supra-natural gifts, resulting in telepathic control over the environment. By a mere act of will-power, they could order hostile sharks about or paralyse their prey so that their working day was reduced to only a few hours.

In this science narrative, the dolphin represents an icon of the type known in cultural history as the noble savage. The marine mammal, constructed here, matches fully the definition of the romanticised savage as 'any free and wild being who draws directly from nature virtues which raise doubts as to the value of civilization' (Fairchild 1961: 2). The dolphin community was thus posited as a Golden Age phenomenon upon which to project the dreams, desires and utopian hopes of members of the 1960-generation. As so often in stories concerning the paradoxical figure of the noble savage, the meanings inscribed in this Soviet dolphin circulate among concepts of Woman-Nature-Native, engendering a textual web of mellow metaphors to counter the harsh imagery of Pavlovism-Stalinism.

The books certainly gave the impression that there already existed a highly-developed, matriarchal and other-wordly dolphin civilization, characterised by little work and much pleasure. A happy, playful, educated and spiritual dolphin community, well-suited, perhaps, to replace both the beast-machine and the austere, terrifying grandfather society of yesterday.

Conclusion

In the Soviet Union, unlike in the West, politics and science were quite openly connected, situated as they were within the phantasmagorical realm of objective truth. Pavlov's 'objective' science served as the legitimisation of Lenin's 'truthful' philosophy of human consciousness. By this manoeuvre, the Pavlovian doctrine became part of the construction of a new, rational society; mirroring man, the harnessed dog was posited as *the* official Aesopian image, *the* metaphor, which trends within the scientific counterculture of the 1960s tried vigorously to eliminate by replacing it with a romanticised and aestheticised Aesopian metaphor of their own.

Their success was, of course, limited. When the government in 1966 banned all commercial killings and catchings of dolphins in the Black Sea for a period of ten years, the move was presented as a very humane and noble step towards 'our sea brothers', the marine mammals. But the nomadic discourse of the regime was as ambiguous as ever. For the main purpose of the moratorium was to instrumentalise, to study and train the by now endangered species for the military, which had been quick to realise the potential of a friendly, intelligent, not to mention speaking, animal. The enlistment of the dolphins in the Red Navy obviously met the fantasies and wishes not of the dolphin state, but of the rocket state.

Notes

1. In the West, the "rat race" has correspondingly become an Aesopian metaphor of human life under capitalism. In the laboratories of Pavlov's American counterpart, the behaviourists, rats had to run through a maze in order to find food – that is, they had to show a pioneering and entrepreneurial spirit.
2. Obviously the greatness of Stalin, acclaimed scientist and philosopher, was hereby likewise legitimised. The most significant part of Vavilov's quotation from Stalin stated that 'the development of the material aspect, the development of the external conditions, *precedes* the development of the ideal aspect, the development of consciousness: first the external conditions change, first the material aspect changes, and *afterwards* consciousness, the ideal side, changes accordingly' (Nauchnaia 1950: 3-4; italics in original).
3. According to Joravsky, to whom I am indebted for this point, Soviet epistemology claimed that 'the laws of higher nervous activity founded on the conditioned reflex (Pavlov's doctrine) show how the human brain generates the knowledge that reflects external reality (Lenin's doctrine)', cf. Joravsky 1989: 388. This became the magic formula in the bonding of Pavlov and Lenin; see also *Bol'shaia Sovetskaia Entsiklopediia*, vol. 31, 1955, p. 519.
4. Pavlov institutionalized the chronic experiment which was conceived as a permanent experiment on (almost) normal and healthy animals although their organism had been changed in one way or another. Before Pavlov, the methods used by physiologists had primarily consisted in

vivisections and acute experiments, resulting in the death of the animals. Pavlov sometimes managed to keep his disfigured dogs alive for years.
5. One of the many fantastic ideas of the celebrated Michurin, 'Father of Apples', is called the agrobiological mentor method; it advocates the hybridization of plants by grafting on a young root-stock a mature scion as so-called 'mentor' or 'educator' (or vice versa, a young scion on an old root-stock). According to Lysenko, this method produced 'good, new and desirable races' (cf. Wetter 1958: 458).
6. Pavlov was also called 'grandfather Pavlov', cf. the reminiscences from 1941, reprinted in Kreps 1967: 199. In a device typical of that time, Pavlov's alleged fondness for children was here used to sustain the familiarity. After World War II, the cult of the *starshinstvo* (priority by force of seniority) evolved into the nationalistic image of the Soviet Union itself as the elder of mankind, cf. Dobrenko 1993: 386.
7. Both during and after his lifetime, Pavlov was considered very religious by the public. His Soviet biographers therefore took great pains to refute this view by putting forward eye-witness evidence of his strong atheism. However, the main point is that each of these two contending discourses in its own way articulates the metaphorical bonding between laboratory and church, scientist and God.
8. Quoted from Cuny 1964: 152; cf. also Nauchnaia 1950: 100 and Pawlow 1953: 544.
9. Shortly before the Session, Stalin had published his letters on linguistics where he maintained that language could not exist outside society.
10. In the early 1980s, echoes of the great dispute were still to be heard in a series of biological studies whose main editor was A. Yablokov, cf. Krushinskaia and Lisitsyna 1983.
11. For an indication of Yablokov's persistence, see his article from 1969.
12. This dolphin icon was recycled in the 1970 U.S. Senate hearings on the Marine Mammal Protection Act. During an impassioned speech on the rights of dolphins, Senator Hubert Humphrey quoted Yablokov as follows: 'Dolphin societies are extraordinary complex, and up to ten generations coexist at one time. If that were the case with man, Leonardo da Vinci, Faraday, and Einstein would still be alive... Could not the dolphin's brain contain an amount of information comparable in volume to the thousands of tons of books in our libraries?' (Crail 1981: 225). Indeed, the dolphin, circulating between the two superpowers, did promote "interspecies" communication. For other Western constructions, see Bryld 1996.

References

Afinogenov, A. (1977) *P'esy, stat'i, vystupleniia. Izbrannoe v dvukh tomakh,* v. 1, Iskusstvo, Moscow.
Babkin, B. P. (1971) *Pavlov. A Biography,* The University of Chicago Press, Chicago-London. (1st edn 1949.)
Bel'kovich, V., S. Kleinenberg and A. Yablokov (1965) *Zagadka okeana,* Molodaia Gvardiia, Moscow.
Bel'kovich, V., S. Kleinenberg and A. Yablokov (1967) *Nash drug – del'fin,* Molodaia Gvardiia, Moscow.
Bryld, M. (1996) 'Dialogues With Dolphins And Other Extraterrestrials: Displacements In Gendered Space', in N. Lykke and R. Braidotti, eds, *Between Monsters, Goddesses And Cyborgs: Feminist Confrontations With Science, Medicine And Cyberspace,* ZED Books, London & New Jersey, pp. 47-71.
Bykov, K. (1948) *I. P. Pavlov – stareishina fiziologov mira. Stenogramma publichnoi lektsii,* Leningrad.
Crail, T. (1981) *Apetalk & Whalespeak. The Quest for Interspecies Communication,* J. P. Tarcher, Inc., Los Angeles.
Cuny, H. (1964) *Ivan Pavlov: The Man And His Theories,* Souvenir Press, London.
Dobrenko, E. (1993) *Metafora vlasti: Literatura stalinskoi epokhi v istoricheskom osveshchenii,* Verlag Otto Sagner, München.
Fairchild, H. N. (1961) *The Noble Savage. A Study in Romantic Naturalism,* Russell & Russell, New York.
Joravsky, D. (1983) 'The Stalinist Mentality and the Higher Learning', *Slavic Review,* Winter, pp. 575-600.
Joravsky, D. (1989) *Russian Psychology,* Basil Blackwell Ltd., Oxford.
Kesarev, V. (1968) 'A chem del'finu dumat'?', *Znanie-sila,* no. 7, pp. 22-24.
Kesarev, V. (1971) 'The inferior brain of the dolphin', *Soviet Science Review,* vol. 2, pp. 52-58.
Kreps, E. M., ed. (1967) *I. P. Pavlov v vospominaniiach sovremennikov,* Nauka, Leningrad.
Krushinskaia, N. and T. Lisitsyna (1983) *Povedenie morskich mlekopitaiushchikh,* Nauka, Moscow.
Lange, K. (1975) *Institut fiziologii imeni I. P. Pavlova. Ocherk istorii organizatsii i razvitiia,* Nauka, Leningrad.
Lilly, J. (1962) 'Kak ia nauchilsia govorit' s moimi del'finami', *Nauka i zhizn',* no. 12, pp. 82-86.
Lilly, J. C. (1962) *Man and Dolphin,* Victor Gollancz, London (1st edn, New York, 1961).
Malaia Sovetskaia Entsiklopediia (1931), vol. 6, pp. 230-231, Moscow.

Nauchnaia Sessiia posviashchennaia problemam fiziologicheskogo ucheniia akademika I. P. Pavlova (1950), Akademiia Nauk SSSR, Moscow-Leningrad.

Panov, E. N. (1980) *Znaki Simvoly Iazyki*, Znanie, Moscow.

Pavlov, I. P. (1951) *Polnoe sobranie sochinenii*, vol. 1, Akademiia Nauk, Moscow-Leningrad.

Pawlow, I. P. (1953) *Sämtliche Werke*, Band III/2, Akademie-Verlag, Berlin.

Tomilin, A. G. (1965) *Istoriia slepogo kashalota*, Nauka, Moscow.

Tomilin, A. G. (1969) *Del'finy sluzhat cheloveku*, Nauka, Moscow.

Tomilin, A. G. (1980) *V mire kitov i del'finov*, Znanie, Moscow.

Tucker, R. C. (1963) *The Soviet Political Mind*, Pall Mall Press, London and Dunmow.

Voronin, L. G. (1970) 'Povedenie "primata" moria – del'fina afaliny Tursiops Truncatus Montagu', *Uspekhi sovremennoi biologii*, vyp. 2, pp. 191-207.

Voronin, L. (1977) *Evoliutsiia vysshei nervnoi deiatel'nosti (ocherki)*, Nauka, Moscow.

Wetter, G. (1958) *Dialectical Materialism*, Greenwood Press, Westport, Connecticut.

Yablokov, A. V. (1969) 'O knige Dzh. Lilli "Mir del'fina"', *Priroda*, no. 5, pp. 61-62.

Evidence of Public Dissent in the Khrushchev Years

ERIK KULAVIG

We were scared – really scared. We were afraid the thaw might unleash a flood, which we wouldn't be able to control and which could drown us.
    Nikita Khrushchev, in *Khrushchev Remembers: The Last Testament.*

We are a minority in a vast country. Abolish the GPU and we are through.
    Yagoda to the American correspondent William Reswich,
    in *I lived Revolution* (1952).

In the course of history several attempts have been made to win the Russian people over to various ideas of revolution or reform, but the result has always been rather poor. This has caused deep frustration and led to the fatal conclusion that the people were reactionary, primitive, uninformed and must therefore be led by some sort of avant-garde. This stereotype of the Russian populace is also amply represented in the ongoing debate on the future of post-Soviet Russia, where both nationalists and Westerners tend to state that the masses must be educated or reeducated to be able to fit into their own very different picture of a new Russian state.

It is widely assumed that the workers' and peasants' traditions and identities as social groups were completely crushed during the reign of Stalin and that they were therefore unable to produce any form of dissent or opposition to the regime. The intelligentsia on the other hand, thanks to its education and the nature of its work, is claimed to have managed to retain its traditions: to have been the moral conscience of society, or to have spoken out for society against the state (Kagarlitskii 1988: 101). I will not dispute the fact that members of the Soviet Russian intelligentsia contributed to the final breakdown of Communism; but I do not believe that the rest of the population were merely defenceless victims of the Party who failed to contribute anything to history. The aim of this chapter is to document the existence of popular dissent and to analyse examples of such dissent in Soviet Russia during the years which came to be known as the "thaw".

State and Society in the Russian Historical Experience

The relation between state and society in Russia's historical experience can best be perceived as one between the conqueror and the conquered. The state was in control, but in the manner of an occupying power dealing with a conquered populace (Tucker 1963: 70). It might be argued that relations were to a certain extent normalised during the second part of the nineteenth century, along with the general modernisation and development of social institutions; but under the Bolshevik regime the notion of a conquered society became as dominant and as real as ever. The sudden and rather non-dramatic collapse of the tsarist regime in 1917 can be interpreted as proof of this particular relationship between state and society. The regime made no real attempt to defend itself. The rulers simply left because they realised they had no supporters. The downfall of the Party-state in 1991 can also be seen as evidence of the fact that society supported the regime only to a very limited extent. In spite of decades of intimidation by the State, in the form of terror and propaganda, society thus proved to have maintained an existence of its own.

In a totalitarian state there are three different positions the population can take towards the alien power of the state. They range from active collaboration (loyalty) through resignation and passive resistance to outright rebelliousness (Tucker 1963: 71). There is almost no doubt that the number of open rebellions or mass unrest against the Party-state in the Soviet Union was relatively insignificant. This does not mean, however, that everything was quiet and peaceful (Alekseeva 1986). Throughout the years of

Soviet power, passive resistance and resignation were a constant cause of concern to the leadership, and eventually the very existence of the regime was threatened. Although the leadership always attempted to suppress information on open and passive resistance and dissent, and to make it less dramatic by acknowledging each instance only as a rare exception to the rule, evidence of passive resistance eventually found its way into the press and public documents. The following example is from the journal *Sovetskoe gosudarstvo i pravo*, 5, 1950:

> A dishonest attitude towards work and towards its obligations, embezzlement, theft and misappropriation of state property and wealth still exist. Various, even leading, workers sometimes endeavour to defraud the state, and permit incorrect information and the submission of untrue reports.

Numerous documents from various Party meetings and congresses were devoted to inveighing against theft, neglect of duty, illicit trade, and criminal bookkeeping. Another indication of passive resistance were the vast resources spent by the state in promoting what in normal countries is taken more or less for granted: loyalty.

The Approach

The fact that the Soviet Union was a totalitarian police state that kept written records on its citizens is, ironically, of great advantage to researchers concerned with the history of Soviet society. These well-guarded archives, kept closed untill recently, reveal an abundance of material reflecting the everyday life, consciousness and behaviour of citizens. This chapter deals with reports from the secret police (KGB), the Ministry of Internal Affairs (MVD) and local Party organisations to various departments of the Central Committee of the CPSU on the atmosphere, attitudes and reactions of the populace to actions taken by the Party or the Government, or to major national or international political events. This system, however incomplete, was meant to serve as an instrument of control as well as an instrument of political feedback for the rulers.

Some Remarks on the State of Soviet Russian Society in the Years Before and Under Khrushchev

The atmosphere of Soviet society after the Second World War was characterised by expectations of new times to come. A notion of freedom *(dukh svobody)* was at work. Its development was due to a certain easing of state control over society during the War and to the experience gained by soldiers at the front. Outer control in the form of fear, repression and alienation was accompanied or replaced by control within the group or by inner control, and there was a discernible shift from a "we" to an "I" identity. The possibilities of horizontal communication between groups of the population who had until then been isolated from each other, helped people to understand the true nature of the regime. In the Red Army, workers, peasants and former prisoners of the Gulag (600,000 of whom were sent to the front in the first months of the war) came together and exchanged information. It should also be mentioned that the soldiers who returned from the West had seen that things were not so bad there after all, and this made them less receptive to anti-western propaganda. This particular atmosphere constituted a unique background for reform of the regime. The notion of freedom was, however, met with new waves of terror, which led to an almost total paralysis of Soviet Russian society towards the end of the forties. This was not fully and openly acknowledged until the death of Stalin, when Khrushchev started revitalising society. Khrushchev's reforms can, however, best be described as a reform of the instruments of control over society and not of the fundamental features of the Soviet regime. The political philosophy underlying it was expressed by the Party Congress in 1956. Very briefly it can be put as follows: If the Party gives you freedom, understood as socialism without Stalinism, and bread, we expect you to work! There is evidence that the reform, together with the ethos expressed by the Party Congress, and the fact that the state started caring about people by improving provision of bread and other commodities, did indeed revitalise vital sections of Soviet Society. This revival, however, lasted only for a short time. After all the system proved unable to satisfy society's expectations, and people lost what little confidence they had gained in the regime during the first years of Khrushchev's reign.

During the 22nd Party Congress in 1961, Khrushchev asked rhetorically whether different opinions could exist under socialism. He himself gave a positive answer, and this marked the starting point for the lively discussions that developed in the sixties. Opposing positions within these discussions were taken by the journals *Novyi Mir and Oktiabr'* headed respectively by Tvardovskii and Kochetov. They were both of communist orientation; but *Novyi Mir* propagated "liberal socialism" à la Khrushchev, while *Oktiabr'* maintained the Stalinist tradition. *Novyi Mir* sided with Khrushchev and *Oktiabr'* with prominent figures such as Molotov and Kaganovich.

Khrushchev might have thought that he had saved the system by releasing prisoners from the camps, saying nice things about the victims and unmasking Stalin at the Party Congresses in 1956 and 1961; but he had not. He had only set in motion a process, which, to his discomfort, gained a momentum of its own. People started asking questions and commenting on practical and political matters. Khrushchev had hoped to put an end to passive resistance and dissent by allowing people to speak and to criticise. When elements of public opinion transgressed the discourse of socialism, however, he started applying the brakes.

When the people understood that the regime was unable to fulfill its promises, signs of frustration began to emerge and a series of so-called "food riots" broke out. Thousands of people openly protested against the Government and the Party. In Voronezh in 1959, and in Kazakhstan in 1960, KGB troops fired at protesting workers and eyewitnesses reported "truckloads of corpses." In 1962, strikes broke out in Novocherkassk and workers from nearby industrial plants marched through the city. Protest meetings were held in front of the headquarters of the Party and the KGB. Troops were directed to the city and again soldiers shot at workers.

Twenty people were killed. Another 12 were sentenced to death at show trials staged immediately after the strikes had been crushed. Hundreds were sent to prison camps.

Russian journalists and historians have claimed that the above-mentioned incidents of open protest constituted only the tip of the iceberg.[1] If the situation had been that dramatic we would probably have learnt more about it, but there is no reason to doubt that protest and dissent were more frequent than we are used to think. In the following sections it is suggested that "food riots" should be interpreted as culminations of a more profound dissatisfaction with the regime.

Examples of Public Dissent

This section deals with reports from local Party organisations and from KGB agents to the Central Committee of the CPSU concerning the political atmosphere within society. Neither type of report should of course be treated as a true reflection of events taking place at the time. Party reports were generally more balanced and less dramatic than KGB reports, which can be explained by the different role played by the two organisations. The Party's role was to take care of propaganda, and dissent was therefore uncomfortable evidence of their failure to achieve their goals. The task of the KGB was to trace anti-Soviet activity; the worse the picture presented therefore, the better for their organisation. One cannot exclude the possibility, moreover, that parts of these documents, or even entire reports were made up by functionaries in order to show their superiors that they were working. The reservations should be borne in mind, when reading the reports, but they do not mean that none of the information is objective. A comparison of the reports from the two organisations enables us to a certain degree to construct a balanced picture.

The two types of reports were constructed along the same pattern. The first part would relate that everything was fine and under control, and that the great majority of the people supported the politics of the Party and the Government. The second part would deal with different forms of dissent, which were always categorised as "insignificant exceptions". The statements were normally documented with citations of what people said at meetings or in private conversations.

If the reports were meant to serve as political feed-back for the rulers, this ritualized format seems rather ineffective; but it was probably inherited from the Stalin period. If dissent was really an exception to the rule, one might wonder why it was given so much consideration, and why such enormous amounts of money and effort were spent on propaganda and control.

In the following section, we will examine three political actions taken by the CPSU in the fifties and early sixties and the reactions to them among the population, as recorded in the type of reports mentioned. The first was a decree on religion of November 10, 1954, which proposed a new and softer line towards religious institutions and believers[2]; the second was a closed letter *(zakrytoe pis'mo)* from the Central Committee of CPSU to party organisations of December 19, 1956, which ordered the latter to take a tougher line towards any kind of dissent[3], and the third was the decree on a rise in prices, issued in May 1962, which fuelled the already significant public dissatisfaction with the rulers and which eventually led to the riots in Novocherkassk in the summer of 1962.[4]

Change of Tactics In Fighting Religion

On 13 November 1954, a decree on religious matters was published, stating that there should be an immediate stop to efforts forcibly to hinder religious belief, and no further administrative interference in church matters. It was also said that any violation of the rights of the clergy or the believers was incompatible with both the Party line and the Constitution. Futhermore it was stated that even among believers there were good citizens who should not be put under suspicion.

In the Kaliningrad oblast, 150 Party agitators organised 150 meetings during the days of the publication of the decree. Their task was to ensure that people gave the decree the right interpretation. As we shall see, this task was not an easy one. From reports to the Central Committee of the CPSU, one can see that the fact that the Party admitted having made a mistake caused considerable bewilderment among the populace. What had been regarded as proper conduct until the day of the decree was now condemned, and vice-versa.

At one of the meetings a kolkhoz-woman was reported to have said:

> The Decree of the Central Committee of the CPSU is fine, but it would have been better if it had come earlier. Instead of telling us why one should not believe in God, they have tried to threaten us into not believing and kept us away from the church by force.[5]

This statement was interpreted as a positive reaction because it proved that the decision to change the party line had been correct. A worker from Omsk obviously did not understand the new signals: 'I live next to the church on Rabinovich Street and I see how the priest is drinking and fooling around. All churches should be closed immediately!'.[6] A statement from a Moslem living in Molotov was recorded as anti-Soviet: 'It is nothing but deceit. They pretend they are doing something good for the people, but it is only meant to rebuff criticism from the West'.[7]

From the reports one learns that churches were well kept, clean and properly heated, while the would-be socialist alternative, workers' clubs, were in a poor state: messy, dirty and unheated. The same went for public registry offices. It is noticeable that this rather evident example of "exit" from official ideology could only be met with poor and ritualised suggestions such as improving the ideological education of club leaders.

The Letter

On 19 December 1956, the Central Committee of the CPSU sent a confidential letter *(zakrytoe pis'mo)* to all party organizations.[8] The heading reads: 'On the strengthening of the political work of the Party among the masses and on the exclusion of anti-Soviet and hostile activity.' The letter contradicted the spirit of the 20th Party Congress that had taken place at the beginning of the year.

The leadership was obviously alarmed by the state of affairs in the country, which was indirectly linked with the social unrest in Hungary and Poland which followed the Congress.

The first part of the letter discussed what was percieved as the growing contradiction between East and West. The reason for this, it was argued, was that the West was upset by the success of socialism and was therefore likely to hit back. To withstand aggression from the West, the Socialist bloc had to reinforce its ideological preparedness. There followed a list of problems that had to be dealt with. Among one of the most serious were the events in Hungary. The uprising was explained solely as the result of foreign infiltration, mainly by the USA. One source, however, indicates that the Soviet leadership knew better. Khrushchev's son-in-law, Adzhubei, writes that Khrushchev understood very well that the uprising in Hungary was a popular one and that he feared the same thing might happen in the Soviet Union (Adzhubei 1989: 153). If this is true, it indicates that there must have been a significant element of dissent within Soviet society and that the leadership and many ordinary people knew that the propaganda about Hungary was fake. Writing about the situation in Russia in 1956, Adzhubei confirms this perception: 'The country was seething. Meetings were organised, extremist calls were heard, someone demanded that the people should be armed. Out of long-standing habit, nobody wrote about this' (Adzhubei 1989: 156).

According to the letter, there were a number of major problems on the internal front that had to be fought. Some Party members had interpreted the 20th Party Congress to mean that action should no longer be taken against dissent and anti-Soviet activity. Such people, the letter said, should be told that they had got it all wrong. Local Party organizations were told to be aware of the fact that certain members of the Party had abused the officially-declared fight against the cult of personality as a means of criticising the Party and promoting the idea of bourgeois democracy. Writers and artists should be told that alien ideas, such as creative freedom, were nothing but expressions of 'rotten liberalism.' The following passage by Lenin was recalled:

Every artist has the right to create freely in accordance with his own ideas, to be totally independent. On the other hand, we are Communists, we cannot allow ourselves to stand on the sideline and watch chaos develop. We must guide this process in accordance with the plan and form its results.[9]

The political leadership was especially alarmed by the conduct of Soviet youth and it was obviously with good reason. A growing tendency towards indifference with regard to political questions was perceived as decadent and dangerous. The significant drop in Komsomol membership including the resignation of existing members, had to be stopped. Anti-Soviet and nationalistic manifestations at institutions of higher education should be fought relentlessly.

It was recommended that the whereabouts and the behaviour of former prison camp inmates should be followed closely. Menshcheviks and bourgeois nationalists were said to bear an especially profound hatred towards the socialist system.

As with the unrest in Poland and Hungary, dissent in the Soviet Union was explained as a result solely of outer or alien ideological factors, rather than internal contradictions or malfunctions within the system itself.

The 20th Party Congress had signalled that faking should no longer serve as a means of creating legitimacy for the regime. This letter, however, testifies to the fact that routines are not so easily replaced, and may be harder to do so in times of crisis.

Judging from the reports to the Central Committee from local Party organisations, a great many members received the message of the closed letter with a feeling of relief. To them, the 20th Party Congress had caused great bewilderment; but in the letter they again found common ground with the leadership. A worker from Leningrad said: 'At last we received clear signals. We must now dispell our petty bourgeois nonchalance and start acting.'[10]

In the following, we will concentrate on what were understood as negative reactions to the letter. A director from Moscow was reported to have said:

> ...if an apparatus was invented that could look through peoples' minds, it would show that 70-80% of our people do not acknowledge the existing order in our country. The 20th Party Congress

loosened the tongues of many people. People bravely started to express their dissatisfaction. This letter, however, is a return to the time before the Congress.[11]

A feeling of disappointment and frustrated hope runs through many of the reports. An engineer from Jaroslavl said the letter was a return to – 'Shut up or we will shut you up.'

A worker in Kuibyshev strongly opposed the idea of the leading role of the Party in literature and art. The result, he said, was already evident: mediocrity and dullness. At the same meeting he said that he had heard on the radio station *Svobodnaia Evropa* that the leader of the great building project where he himself was employed had received 50,000 rubles and a big car. The local Party Bureau did not take any action against the worker mentioned, and it was later removed.

Kozyrev, who was a Government employee, was reported as having said:

> We are discussing the problems of political agitation but we do not see the most important thing. The decisions of the 20th Party Congress are only talked about, nobody does anything. We only have democracy on paper... We are still afraid to criticize because we still cannot rule out that we will end up in prison... We should look towards Yugoslavia and Hungary and learn from them how to build socialism.[12]

We learn that Kozyrev later regretted his dissent. He told the Party Committee that he had been drunk and was eventually forgiven.

The Youth

The growing political apathy of youth was of great concern to the leadership. Judging from the reports, the concern was justified. A student from Kursk said at a meeting at the university: 'Komsomol is a boring organization. They only demand work and study. There is no joy, no fun. It may all end as in Hungary. I demand freedom for young people.'[13] There is other evidence that young people felt an almost instinctive animosity towards the authorities and the control they exercised, and, of course, tried to avoid any kind of interference in their lives by the state. The majority did so passively. Passive resistance was, however, in some way more dangerous to the regime than open rebellion, as the culprit could not so easily be detected and arrested (Burg 1961).

At a meeting at the Institute of Forestry a student from Briansk said:

> The Soviet Union will never overtake the capitalist countries. The Soviet Union has not improved upon the conditions of the Russian peasant. And, while the workers in the USA can buy a car, an engineer in the USSR dare not even dream of getting one. The standard of living in the USSR is below the level of subsistence.[14]

At Molotov State University, a student at a Komsomol meeting said:

> 'You are all cowards and hypocrites. In the corners you whisper that communism is nothing but a new religion, but here you are silent'.[15]

At a conference on the history of the CPSU at the same university, a student asked the lecturer: 'Will the events in Hungary trigger a counterrevolution in the USSR?' The lecturer replied: 'No!' The student: 'That's a pity' *(A zhal')*.[16]

At a seminar on history, the students Eisfeld and Baranov presented a paper in which they stated that the cult of personality was a consequence of the mono-party system, and drew a comparison between Hitler's Germany and Stalin's Soviet Union. The only safeguard against the cult of personality, they stated, was a responsible Government and freedom of speech. The author of the report wrote: 'Eisfeld and Baranov support so-called Western democracy in opposition to our Soviet system. They claim that a political leader can only gain authority in a multi-party system'.[17]

May 1962

In May 1962, the Soviet Government raised the prices of meat, milk and butter by 30%. From an economic point of view this was a rational action, but politically it was a mistake. In a public decree the Party tried to explain to the people that the action taken by the Government was justified. But their efforts were apparently in vain, at least as regards part of the population.

In the summer of 1962, the leader of the KGB reported to the Central Committee that anti-Soviet activity had grown significantly in the first months of the year and especially after the above-mentioned price rise. Some 7,705 anti-Soviet posters and leaflets, produced by 2,522 authors, had been detected. That was 100% more than in the same period during the previous year. Most activity was traced in the Ukraine, Azerbajdzhan, Georgia, Latvia, Stavropol, Krasnoiarsk, Rostov, Leningrad and Moscow. According to the report, the written material contained malicious attacks on individual leaders of the CPSU, slander, nationalistic statements, and a lack of belief in the building of communism in the USSR. Some of the material envinced hatred towards the CPSU and towards Communists. Threats towards local leaders were expressed.

As a result of the industrious activity of the KGB, the report stated, 1089 authors of 6,726 anti-Soviet documents had been caught. Among them were 364 workers (35%), 192 employees, 210 students and school children, 108 with no occupation, 105 pensioners and 60 kolkhoz members. It was stated that only 40 had any higher or intermediate education, which means that more than half came from the least educated part of the population. Perhaps more surprisingly, no fewer than 89 were candidate members of the CPSU and 116 were members of Komsomol.[18]

Novocherkassk

In Novocherkassk, big strikes broke out in May 1962 and workers marched towards the city, where they were met by firearms. The leadership expended great efforts on isolating these events. Obviously, they feared that the riots would spread to other regions. Troops surrounded the city and the industrial plants. As long as the conflict lasted, no one was allowed to enter or to leave the city. On the day of the shooting, the all Union radio programme aired a concert which, so they said, was transmitted from the central square of Novocherkassk. An engineer, who was living next to the central square told afterwards that he was looking out of his window and saw nothing but armoured cars and soldiers (Bespalov 1989).

Judging from the reports on peoples' reactions to the price rises, the concern of the political leadership was justified. Let us take a closer look at what was recorded by the KGB and sent to the Central Committee. The recorded statements can be divided into three subgroups: radical protest, unmasking the Soviet system, and sarcasm. Let us first look at some examples from the first group. An employee at the Vnukovo airport, Lapin, said at a meeting:

'Let's march to Red Square and demand that they cancel the decree on the price rises.'[19] At a meeting at the Petrovsk metal plant where the price rise was discussed the worker Timofeev said : 'One should have a machine gun and shoot them down. All of them'.[20] A carpenter in Riazan said to the party agitator: 'This is it! Everybody should be shot one after the other. And we should begin with you'.[21]

Some examples of statements unmasking the Soviet system: A worker from Smolensk said at a meeting: 'We have no democracy in the USSR. That is why the Government does as it pleases. If workers were not stupid, they would organise strikes as they do in the West.'[22] Mikhailovna, who worked at the Pavletskii Railway station, said: 'It was wrong to cut down the private sector. If they had allowed the workers and the peasants to keep their cattle, we would have had enough meat'.[23] An engineer, Mestechkin, said: 'Is it really true, that it was impossible to restore agriculture in the period which has passed since he (Stalin) died? It is not. The crisis has deeper roots, but it seems that they should not be talked about'.[24] The honoured artist Zaslavskii said: 'We are not going to die from this, but we should be ashamed. I wish they had kept quiet about us overtaking America. It is repulsive day in and day out to listen to the loudspeakers saying: "We, we, we." All this is nothing but boundless boasting'.[25]

A technician from the "Pochtovyi iashchik" plant in Moscow said: 'How can we trust official statements when we are told at lectures on the international situation that rumours about price increases in the USSR are nothing but hostile propaganda spread by BBC radio, which just proves that the BBC was right?'[26]

The following two statements are examples of sarcasm: A worker from Leningrad: 'Life is getting worse. Kennedy would be doing the right thing if he dropped the bomb on the USSR'.[27] 'Eat grass, meat isn't necessary'.[28]

After Novocherkassk, the KGB and MVD were ordered by the Central Committee to intensify surveillance at production plants and universities, and to report regularly to the Central Committee. This action certainly contradicted the spirit of the 20th Party Congress, and it was a clear sign of concern in the leadership as to where society was moving.[29]

Conclusions

The various reports to the Central Committee demonstrate that Soviet Society was reviving in the "liberal years" of the fifties and early sixties. Independent horizontal communication, which had never been totally absent in Soviet society, expanded and even vertical communication, from society to the state, emerged in form of protests, demonstrations and even riots. This tells us that public dissent was desperately seeking an outlet. Widespread passive resistance, which was directly documented by for example low productivity, and indirectly by the enormous amounts of effort and money spent by the regime on telling people how they should behave and on controlling society, provides further indication that there was no peace between the Party, State and society.

Dissent was moreover not a monopoly of the intelligentsia. We have seen that also ordinary people were aware of the injustice and the absurdities of the regime and they reacted accordingly. This is an important fact to take into account when one is looking for explanations as to why the Soviet system did reform after all and why it eventually broke down. It might also shed some light on the gloomy picture of the prospects for the "new Russia".

Notes

1. Kozlov, V. A., ed. (1993) *Neizvestnaia Rossiia*, Istoricheskoe nasledie, Moscow.
2. 'Ob oshibkakh v provedenii nauchno-ateisticheskoi propagandy sredi naseleniia.' (1959)
3. 'Zakrytoe pis'mo TsK KPSS k partijnym organizatsiiam, ob usilenii politicheskoi raboty partiinykh organizatsii v massakh i peresechenii antisovetskikh, vrazhdebnykh elementov.' (1956), TsKhSD, f.89, op.6, d.2, ll. 1-13.
4. 'O povyshenii zakupochnykh tsen na krupnyi rogatyi skot, svinei, ovets, ptitsu, maslo zhivotnoe i slivki i roznichnykh tsen na miaso, miasnye produkty i maslo zhivotnoe.'
5. 'O pervykh otklikakh trudiashchikhsia na postanovlenie TsK KPSS ''Ob oshibkakh v provedenii nauchno-ateisticheskoi propagandy sredi naseleniia." (1954), TsKhSD, f.5, op.32, d.12, ll. 1-12.
6. ibid.
7. ibid.
8. 'Zakrytoe pis'mo TsK KPSS k partijnym organizatsiiam, ob usilenii politicheskoi raboty partijnykh organizatsii v massakh i peresechenii antisovetskikh, vrazhdebnykh elementov.' (1956), TsKhSD, f.89, op.6, d.2, ll. 1-13.
9. ibid
10. 'O khode obsuzhdenia pisma TsK KPSS "ob usilenii politicheskoi raboty partijnykh organizatsij v massakh i peresechenii antisovetskikh, vrazhdebnykh elementov v partijnykh organizatsiiakh RSFSR.' (1957), TsKhSD, f.5, op. 32, d. 77, ll. 1-30.
11. ibid.
12. ibid.
13. ibid.
14. ibid.
15. ibid.
16. ibid.
17. ibid.
18. V. Semichastnyi, KGB to the Central Committee on anti-soviet activity. July 25, 1962,TsKhSD, f. 89, op.51, d.1.
19. KGB to the Central Committee. TsKhSD, f.89,op.6, d. 13.
20. ibid.
21. ibid.
22. ibid.
23. ibid.

24. ibid.
25. ibid.
26. ibid.
27. ibid.
28. ibid.
29. "Ob usilenii bor'by organov gosudarstvennoi bezopasnosti s vrazhdebnymi proiavleniami antisovetskikh elementov." Voprosy KGB, Prokuratury SSSR 1962. F.89, op.6, d.20, ll. 1-16. TsKhSD.

References

Adzhubei, A. (1989) *Te desiat' let*, Sovetskaia Rossiia, Moscow.
Alekseeva, L. (1986) *Mass Unrest in the USSR*, ARL, Pentagon Library.
Bespalov, J. and V. Konovalov (1989) 'Novocherkassk 1962', in L. A. Kirshner *Svet i teni velikogo desiatiletiia*, Lenizdat, Moscow.
Burg, D. (1961) 'Observations on the Soviet University Students', in R. Pipes *The Soviet Intelligentsia*, Columbia University Press, New York.
Genis, A. and P. Vail (1988) *60-e. Mir sovetskogo cheloveka*, Ardis, Ann Arbor.
Gerner, K. and S. Hedlund (1989) *Ideology and Rationality in the Soviet Model. A Legacy for Gorbachev*, Routledge, London.
Kagarlitskii, B. (1988) *The Thinking Reed. Intellectuals and the Soviet State from 1917 to the Present*, London.
Miliukov, P. N. (1905) *Russia and Its Crisis*, The University of Chicago Press, London.
Tucker, R. (1963) *The Soviet Political Mind*, Praeger, London.

On the Cognitive-Normative Mapping of Soviet Civilization: The Space Beneath

Natal'ia Kozlova

Recently, a number of researchers have analysed Soviet society as a species of civilization (Kotkin 1995). There exists a growing need to elaborate a map of this civilization. There are many possible ways and methods of doing this. One could engage in a search for "essentials" and "basic regularities". Another possibility, however, is to penetrate to the heart of the epoch through an examination of "insignificant" surface symptoms, e.g., by observing street life or reading human documents.

The present chapter belongs to the second branch of research and is an attempt to reconstruct the specific features of Soviet social life manifested in one particular source.

Notes by Evgeniia Grigor'ievna Kiseleva

This study is based on research into personal notes written by an ordinary woman, Evgeniia Grigor'ievna Kiseleva, whose manuscript is deposited at the Documentation Centre, 'The People's Archive'. The manuscript is part of a collection containing the writings and memoirs of private citizens.[1]

The notes were written over a period of thirteen years. Writing was started after 1977 and completed prior to 1990. Kiseleva was born on 1 November 1916 in the *khutor* (small-holding) of Novozvanovka, in the Popasn'anskii district of the Voroshilovgrad (Lugansk) region. She lived almost all her life in the town of Pervomaiskii in the same region. It was there that she died on 27 September 1990. Now the town belongs to the Donbass region of Ukraine, a major coal-mining area in the former USSR.

Her story is a common one: in her childhood and youth she lived a rural life, moving in 1932 to a town, where she fell in love and got married in 1933, giving birth to two sons who were born, respectively, in 1935 and 1941. Then came the war, the death of her father and mother right before her eyes, and a period in hiding (for several months she was trapped on the front-line between Nazis and Soviets engaged in military action). Subsequently she survived her husband's vanishing into the blue and the ensuing struggle for existence, followed by another bad marriage which nevertheless lasted for twenty years before eventually breaking up. After her 'emancipation', there followed more hard work, strained relations with relatives, the hand-to-mouth existence of a pensioner, the problems of children and grandchildren, and so on and so forth. In other words an ordinary life, typical of the Soviet period of Russia's history.

Her immediate milieu consisted of mining families, former country folk. She occupied one of the lowest steps on the social scale. Lack of cultural and social capital (Bourdieu 1990) meant that she was constrained to stay in one place and that her scope for social mobility was extremely narrow. Her first and last habitats lay in the closest geographical proximity: a mere 15 kilometres separated the khutor from the semi-urban miners' settlement.

Kiseleva's education consisted in five years at a rural Ukrainian-language school. She first started "writing for herself" at the age of 63. Her writing was full of spelling mistakes, and its manner could be called "naive" by analogy with naive painting. In reading it, there can be no mistaking the writer's low social status.

The "nethermost" spaces of Soviet civilization remain practically uninvestigated. In the first place, monological official discourse disregarded subjects of this kind. Research relating to the so-called 'culture of poverty' was not carried out in the USSR. The lifestyles and social games of the lower classes seem to have been located right "in the blind spot" of Soviet vision. This *terra incognita* was easy prey for all sorts of ideological and political speculations.

In the second place, written documents which reflect the world view of the lower classes "from within" are quite rare. Those who inhabit the margins of society generally fail to gain admittance to the world of writing. In committing her thoughts to paper, Kiseleva appears to have ushered the student into a non-verbalised universe, thus opening it up for discourse. The following is an attempt to interpret Kiseleva's notes from the point of view of social and civilizational properties.

A World Where Everyone Knows Everyone

Kiseleva's community is a world where everyone knows everyone. Lack of room, cramped space and over-population can be felt almost physically. All destinations are a short distance away. Everyone around is familiar with the details of other people's personal lives.

Whatever happens, one is always tightly encircled by those who know the situation and command an easy "understanding of things". A person whom you think you do not know turns out to be an acquaintance of your friends or relatives.

> When I arived in Kalinovo in the middle of the night with the kids I get down off the cart and go up to the first hut I come to and knock on the door, and turns out I know the folks there allready... (Когда я приехала сриди ночи с детьми в Калиново слезла из брички и пошла до первой попавшей хаты постучала к людям, эти люди оказалися знакомые мне...) (TsDNA, f. 115, d. 1, l. 10-11).

The circle of relatives is vast. 'Relatives' are all those who are blood kin, including cousins, second cousins, second cousins twice (and more) removed, etc. This category also includes husbands – a 'kin husband' (i.e. the first, beloved one) and a 'non-kin husband' (i.e. her second one). Habits and customs are held sacred. It's shameful not to take part in funeral rites even though you may have quarelled with the person now being buried 'for the rest of his life'. Neighbours participate actively in all the ups and downs of one's family life; they would know, for instance, how a dead body was dressed for a funeral and exactly what garments it was wearing.

People in power also belong to your own flock: the authorities' representatives are everybody's acquiantances: 'The police cheif Nikolai Ivanovich Pomazuev droped in with Nikolai Stipanovich Shavovarov and Timofei Liakhov' ('зашли начальник милиции Помазуев Николай Иванович, Шароваров Николай Стипанович и Ляхов Тимофей') (TsDNA, f. 115, d. 1, 1. 78-79).

The social circle is narrow, and nets of interaction are tight. Suppose one tries to draw a map of Kiseleva's life-space, what should be plotted on it? Houses where relatives and neighbours live, a food store and a marketplace, a hospital and a graveyard. Also, a police station *(militsia)* and 'a third street', a local Inferno where seduced souls descend from grace: unfaithful husbands, women of lax morals, and those who have served a term in a prison camp. It is only in the second half of Kiseleva's life that a savings bank and a television make their appearance on the map.

Again and again, one gets the impression that the life Kiseleva describes is going on somewhere outside the system of universal social relations, and that her community is excluded from any more extensive system of social ties. Segmented organic bonds obviously prevail over functional and mechanical ones.

Kiseleva's main field of interaction is restricted to the minicommunity. The reader of the document learns much about the life of this mini-community: eating and sleeping habits, three-shift work schedules and the traditional cycles of peasant culture, its weekdays and holidays, births and funerals, etc. New Year and birthday parties, Easter and Christmas celebrations go hand in hand with official holidays like the 8th of March and the 1st of May. One learns about the life in a peasant *izba* (hut), in a fivestorey block or communal barracles, as well as about love and marriage, childbirth, fate and destiny, outdoor lavatories and sexual behaviour. And, of course, about ritual feasts and favourite dishes: pies, *borshch*, and so forth: 'Holy eggs and soup with buckwheat and a tin of fish I opend, salt cucumbers and slised Easter cake'; 'lots of vodka and home-brew of corse' ('яички свяченые, суп с гречкой и роспичатала рыбную консерву, соленые огурци, паска нарезаная', 'много водьки и конечно самогончик') (TsDNA, f. 115, d. 2, I. 64, 15).

The nature of social bonds suggests that Kiseleva belongs to a traditional, or semi-traditional, type of community. At any rate, the stories she tells of her childhood and early youth obviously derive from such a society. This impression is confirmed both by the documents I have read and by statistical data (Zaionchkovskaia 1991; Rybakovskii 1988; Vishnevskii 1992).

Transitivity

Kiseleva's stories concerning her life in the workers' settlement give evidence of a different type of society in which features of traditional community are nevertheless very strong. The text abounds in evidence of transitivity – both at an individual level and in the society as a whole.

Members of Kiseleva's community believe in sorcery and the evil eye. Archaic magic rites continue to be an inseparable part of their semi-urban lifestyle. Kiseleva can easily read the meaning of the following message: 'The next day we gets up in the morning and there on the doorstep theres this stone cross and a small crowbars bin put there I says to Mitia go and take a look theres grattitude for you' ('Нафторой день устаем утром у нас на порок выложен крест из камню и положин ломик говорю Митя иди посмотры какая нам благодарность') (TsDNA, f. 115, d. 1, l. 55). The cross designates threat.

Omens and tokens function as a means of interpretating everyday interaction and as a means of legitimising one's own actions. While visiting her son at his place, Kiseleva sees her daughter-in-law sweeping the floor in her – that is, Kiseleva's – presence. Folklore holds such conduct to be a sign of 'sweeping a guest out of one's place', and accordingly Kiseleva interprets the younger woman's actions as a signal that she, the mother-in-law, is an unwanted guest in the house. Kiseleva's writing gives evidence of numerous stereotypes that can be traced back to traditional peasant culture.

At the same time, however, the notes register the step-by-step process of mastering new "living devices", the new vehicles of activity and communication by which modernity gradually permeates everyday life.

In the society described by Kiseleva, the domain of privacy has not yet taken shape. Here, an individual is never left alone. Being alone is perceived as a form of suffering. Privacy as a social value does not yet seem to have evolved. A fragment about television (Kiseleva spells it with a capital T, *Televizor*) is of great interest:

> Solitudes a terible thing, specialy when its misty and rainy, too damp for going out and you cant jist sit home, thank God for the man who thougt up the Television and the radio. I turn on the radio for starters but then I turn on the Television and its talking to the hole room seems to be shouting here there and evrywhere, Ive got all these people in the room and then they put this concert on the Telly, songs and dances I started singing along, oh little little box, the one about the pedlers it realy cheered me up I was puling out all the old songs I know, solitudes a coffin with music, specialy in wintertime.
> (Одиночество страшное дело, а тут еше погода туман дошь, сыро непойти куданибуть, ни в комнате сидеть, да спасибо человека который выдумал Телевизор, радиво. Я включила радиво этого мало, я включила и Телевизор говорить на всю комнату кричит и там и там как бутто-бы, у меня в комнате много людей да еше по Телевидению передавали концерт песни и танци хоровые я стала подпивать, ох лехка лехка коробушка "коробейники" и мне стало весело на душе какую знаю песню подтягиваю одиночество это гроб с музикой, а тем более зимнее время) (TsDNA, f. 115, d. 2, 1. 62).

The television seems to bring the writer back to the parties *(posidelki)* of her youth in the village. A sleepless night alone with a blank sheet of writing paper is apparently Kiseleva's first ever experience of privacy.

All the personal notes and memoirs that I've read by ordinary Soviet people, especially those written by the generation born between 1910 and 1920, almost invariably contain a description of the staggering impression made by seeing a train for the first time in one's life. In the case of Kiseleva this experience took place in the 1940s, when our heroine took a train to go to a big city, Kiev. It was there that she first saw a telephone too. By the end of her life the telephone was already an item of her everyday reality. Comparisons between "now" and "then" often occur in her notes.

As can be seen from the notes, the life of many Soviet people was lived "on the edge". Kiseleva records war and famine, tuberculosis, the death of her brothers (one killed in action, the other in German captivity), the death of her parents. In fact, Death is an important actor in the drama of Soviet history. Survival is the crucial aim and the central value. Kiseleva is, in the first place, a person who has managed to outlive others, who has emerged victorious from numerous life-threatening situations. Perhaps this was her motivation for writing down her recollections, and I imagine that the same motive must have guided many others who eventually became "naive" writers of this kind. The memoirs of Soviet people are not simply those of old-timers who, having completed the process of "life construction", have lost interest in the future. These writers are above all survivors. Their life experience tells them that any means are justified by the end of survival.

The peace-time urban life of the 1960s, 1970s and 1980s seems a miracle in comparison with war-time and Kiseleva's childhood years in the village. One senses that Soviet society was able to retain stability as long as there were people alive who could recall and bear witness. It began gradually to decline as such people one by one departed this world, quitting the social arena to give way to new generations and new social games.

External Control vs. Self-Control

The people who surround Kiseleva are not accustomed to using a handkerchief and sometimes relieve themselves in full sight of everybody. From the point of view of a "cultured person", they seem to command no self-control, appear to have had no training in patience, and show abrupt changes of mood from empathy and compassion to violent aggression, both verbal and physical. They can easily endure pain and as readily inflict pain on others.

Especially worthy of researchers' attention are the surprising contrasts in behaviour and the general emotional imbalance described. Everyday conflicts are habitually settled by means of violence – natural, immediate, unrestrained and "unlicensed". Hell-raising and fighting as a means of everyday conflict-resolution are familiar episodes of Soviet (and post-Soviet) life. One feels that for the antagonistic parties this is a significant method of emotional relaxation. Not so much that they derive sadistic pleasure from the sight of others' sufferings; rather, these fights are a form of managed emotional release. In any case, emotional self-control appears to be extremely low.

Conflicts are easily initiated, "all of a sudden", as though for no obvious reason. In one episode we see neighbours peacefully playing cards in the yard, when all of a sudden a fight begins, blows are exchanged, teeth knocked out, and so on (see TsDNA, f. 115, d. 2, 1. 69-70 et al.). Numerous similar examples could be found.

One might ask how such conflicts could be interpreted at all. I believe that Norbert Elias' anthropological model might usefully be applied here (Elias 1978a and 1978b; 1982). According to Elias, the capacity for self-control among the members of a society, which exists in parallel with external forms of control over social nets and interpersonal links, is a significant criterion of the civilizational development of the given society (Elias 1978b: 156-157). Thus one can trace connections between social structures and a social person. The document under analysis appears susceptible to this kind of research.

Emotional imbalance, sudden switches from joy to sorrow, from love to hatred, from tranquillity to irritation are not a matter of temper but rather a social feature. In the social space described in Kiseleva's notes, the degree of self-control and self-restriction is low. The ability to suppress affects for the sake of purpose-oriented behaviour is practically non-existent; indeed, one can hardly speak of the presence of rationality at all. That people lack self-control over their affects is not the only problem. Another symptom of rationality, namely postponed gratification, is also absent. Kiseleva's husband is incapable of saving up a bonus awarded to him for many years of work: 'We bougt a pig ready for eating and cut it up, our frends didnt leave the house till theyd eaten the hole pig' ('купили кабана уже готового кормяшего зарезали, друзя не выходили из хаты пока не сьели усего кабана') (TsDNA, f. 115, d. 2, 1. 53-54).

Many of the dangers that threaten Kiseleva and other people around her are of an imminent physical nature: famine, poverty, violent death. The absence of any sense of ontological safety is not conclusive to self-control. The people we meet on the pages of Kiseleva's manuscript are not "pacified". The life of the lowest strata of semi-urban dwellers shows a high degree of open aggression. There were vast spaces in Soviet society where this applied, and it still holds true in vast areas of post-Soviet social reality.

The urban and semi-urban life led by Kiseleva's community in her adult life should not be contrasted, in this respect, to the traditional rural milieu which she experienced in her childhood. Her own texts testify, on the contrary, to the fact that her rural life was a far cry from the harmonious unity and solidarity described by researchers from Toennis to Redfield. The Russian scholar M. M. Gromyko (Gromyko 1986, 1991) also depicts the rural community as a harmonious and pacified locus, where people and social functions are well-adjusted to one another, and where conflicts are "imported" from beyond. Thus, several researchers explicitly state or seem implicitly to believe that such communities were unlikely to develop and modernise so long as friendly relations and a sense of unity were better maintained there that they were in larger modern societies.

In fact, the problem turns out to be more involved and more "multi-layered" than this suggests. A pronounced instability in human relations can be perceived in traditional communities as well. Kiseleva's recollections of her early years in the village contain many references to severe conflicts in the family. "Writing on the body" is the principal method of child training. It is from physical punishment that a child will get knowledge about what she may and what she must not do. Among children, the micro-level balance of power is also established through physical violence: a child get the upper hand only by beating his adversary. Pacification is nevertheless achieved through mechanisms inherent in traditional society, i.e. through rites and habits, the power of community opinion. In this respect traditional communities can be regarded as highly civilised, since they command well-tested and efficient tools of conflict management.

In the new, semi-urban community of neighbours, these instruments no longer work. Kiseleva's notes give us insight into how traditional society was undermined from beneath, from those very layers that it should have rested upon. What was unthinkable now becomes possible. Thus tradition mandates that a daughter-in-law should obey her mother-in-law by doing certain kinds of her chores about the house and, in general, 'showing respect'. When the clamp of custom that holds life together is removed, daughters-in-law cease to obey. No substitute for this traditional subordination can be found at any new level of relations, so it simply comes to an end. Conflicts tend thus to get more ferocious and uncontrollable:

> Nikolai lived with his mother, he got marryed and took himself a wife called Pasha and got himself four children by her, she beat up her mother-in-law and made fun of her the village counsil went in and devided things up Pasha dragged the mum away from her plate of soup and stamped on her head with her heals (Николай жил сней с матерю, и женился и взял сибе жену Пашу, у которой прижито четверо детей, она свекруху била издевалася сельсовет приезжал делил Паша отсаживала мать от тарелки супа, била маму каблуками по голове) (TsDNA, f. 115, d. 2, 1. 32-33).

Community public opinion still exists but has lost its pacifying and civilising power.

From a socio-cultural aspect, Kiseleva's writing is a lament over the disappearance of traditional values. Her own conduct is guided by practical schemata prescribing a certain order of operations, specific principles of hierarchy and division, and indeed an entire vision of the social world (Barthes 1970; Bourdieu 1990). These principles stem from her incorporated peasant past, but she constantly runs into situations in which these principles fail to work, her competence in communication is nullified and her cultural codes will prove impossible to apply in practice. For Kiseleva, the code of traditional culture is perceived as the only "natural" imperative: within it she feels at home. However, the proverbs that express "folk wisdom" and which serve, alongside other forms of knowledge, as the main instrument of orientation in a traditional community, can both fail her – and help her. Order is not maintained, and problems of communication arise. In general Kiseleva's notes can be interpreted as a history of the collapse of traditional values, habits, order, and social harmony: there is nothing to substitute for these. Or at least, any new code seems questionable.

There also exist more complicated means of reconciliation. As we know, the Soviet law-court was understood by "the broad masses" not as a legal space for conflict resolution but as the locus of punishment. 'For the sake of our peace and happiness the Procurator raised his bloody hand' – ('Прокурор на наше счастье и покой поднял окровавленные руки') – is a piece of urban folklore. Preference is obviously given to "judgement by truth and conscience" rather than to official legal procedures. People do not know what the word "Law" means, but they intuitively perceive that no such thing exists.

The jail, the prison camp, the *zona* are significant elements of everyday life, are invariably "with us", invisibly (or visibly) present:

> I glanced at the entranse to his house and saw this car standing there the Bodywork was cuvered over I thougt its the Black Maria come for him, my hart was on fire, oh my God, I went and put on my glasses came out on the balcany took a look and its was just a brake-down veicle I carmed down a bit and felt releved (глянула возле его подезда стоить машина, критая Будка я думала черный Ворон за ним приехала, уменя огнем палохнуло серце, ой Боже мой, пошла надела очки вышла на балкон россмотрелася а то аварийная машина немножко отошла Успокоялася) (TsDNA, f. 115, d. 2, 1. 83).

When people find themselves caught up in centralised systems of violence, they will do their best to avoid an open clash with the state by simple domestic measures. It is worth mentioning that, besides immediate physical "punishment", community members use specific forms of trade and exchange, giving away money, or a coat, or an accordion. They grant each other forgiveness, celebrating this event by a shared repast and a drinking party.

Methods of Survival

Kiseleva's community uses approved social techniques and patterns which are most vividly represented in everyday peasant resistance (Scott 1985).

The value of equality is cultivated here not so much as everybody's right to equal distribution, but rather as the right of each and every individual to existence. One can see that a variety of moral economy is preserved here, something akin to the peasants' habit of *kusochki* (morsels) when a hungry neighbour could be given a morsel from the family's last loaf of bread (Engel'gardt 1987: 56-60). This is a case of a traditional custom built into the body as a function of collective survival. In fact, it offers an incorporated history of peasantry.

Again, one comes across numerous, multi-functional social ties that are driven by personal confidence among individuals. Kiseleva's notes abound in episodes showing such mutual aid: she saved the life of a wounded soldier during the war and helped starving miners in 1933 (cheating at a miners' canteen that employed her). Once she helped a woman who, in her turn, had saved Kiseleva's life when they shared potatoes that the woman had stolen from a kolkhoz.

The interpretation of such practices is hindered by certain methodological difficulties. One might be tempted to believe that such modes of behaviour were governed by high morality, the "spirituality" allegedly present in community members which leads them to obey a moral imperative and resist power. But what they, in fact, obey, unconsciously, is a social taboo, an implicit norm. They have techniques of co-operative survival pre-built into their bodies. This idea is confirmed by my own experience of reading human documents.

Thus, Kiseleva's body "carried" implicit knowledge of and skills in fail-safe survival practices, and she conformed to the rules involved even during the periods of relatively tolerable existence. She would knit rugs and sell them at the marketplace, she 'lived on botles Id give them in and that gave me a bit of extra on top of my wages and then Id put my wages in the savings bank' (' жила бутилками здаю вот мне и добавок к зарплате а свою зарплату я ложила на книжку сберегательную') (TsDNA, f. 115, d. 3, I. 20).

As said above, Kiseleva's text is a lament for collapsing traditional values. At an anthropological level this collapse manifests itself differently in males and females. A married woman does everything she can to follow the traditional ethical code of marriage. In men, this code is seen to have been destroyed. It's the women who reproduce traditional values and thus guarantee the preservation of life of the community. While men drink all their earnings away, women keep up the life of the family, working in the kitchen-garden, keeping hens, and maintaining domestic food stocks. In Russian culture the woman is perceived as base matter, the chaos on which males are expected to imprint order. But the picture presented in Kiseleva's writing is the reverse: a man is a destroyer, the bearer of chaos, while a woman is the generator of order and the bearer of the pacifying fundamentals of civilization. The men depicted in her notes seem indifferent to survival: their inherent survival instinct no longer works but it is wholly preserved in women.

The new world is a 'vodka world' (*vodochnyi mir*). Members of this community know only too well the medical symptoms of chronic alcoholism:

> I says to him if you drink any more vodka your going to compleetly ruin your lungs, your going to have the runs the hole time and ruin your blader and then you wont be able to hold your water, remember Granny Zhenia now, itll be like it was with D. I. Grandad Tiurichev your adopted Grandad (я ему говорю побольше пей водки, совсем испалиш лехкые, и желудок всегда будиш поносить, и испалиш мочевой вот тогда не будет держатся моча, вот тогда вспомниш Бабушку Женю, так будит как у Д.И. Деда Тюричева твоего Деда Неродного...) (TsDNA, f. 115, d. 3, 1. 5-6).

In modern societies, there exists an unparalleled variety of leisure practices. Most of them, including sports, serve not only for relaxation and the appropiate channelling of affects and libidinous energies, but also offer possibilities of non-aggressive excitement. Kiseleva's community, at the time of writing, had not delineated a social domain of leisure that could be used for the management of affects, that were otherwise uncontrollable. There is not a single mention of sports or games. Even holidays as occasions for relaxation and compensation practically disappear. Soviet red-letter days and religious holidays are held sacred, but degenerate into drinking bouts. Alcohol is seen as the only means of compensation available.

It should be noted that "rude" people like Kiseleva's protagonists (and like herself, as she believes) are whole-hearted people. Since they have no claims to prestige, they should command a larger than usual range of affect resolution techniques. Kiseleva takes life as it is. Some scholars argue that the culture of poverty is hedonistic in its essence. The text under analysis seems to confirm this point of view. Joy is not too frequent here, but the sense of the completeness and richness of life is experienced to the full. The cup of life brims over with pleasure.

Mini-Community and Big Society: New Codes?

It has already been mentioned that the community depicted in the notes gives the impression of a life lived far off the beaten track of History. In fact, however, life there goes on within the framework of the state and the society at large, and is consequently intertwined with the wider system of functional bonds. It remains under the pressure of the state from outside, from the state-run educational system, and from other social groups. Let us look at how the attributes of the larger society enter the life of this mini-community, bearing in mind what has already been said elsewhere concerning the role of mass communication.

The names of the political leaders of the time are practically absent in Kiseleva's manuscript. Lenin's name appears twice, as part of a saying. Stalin is mentioned once, and only in connection with the war: he was 'kind and trustful' ('милостив и доверчив'), and couldn't have suspected that Hitler was an 'igoist of human existence' ('игаист человеческого сушествования') (TsDNA, f. 115, d. 2, 1. 12).

22 June 1941 is the only historic date noted by Kiseleva, in connection with the date of birth of her younger son. Too many things are perceived as if through a historical fog: 'Either its revolution or its War' ('толи революция то ли Война').

The event of world history constantly referred to in the recollections of "cultured" writers are entirely absent in Kiseleva's text. She explains in passing why she was trying to write dates in detail and in the full form: it was because she had been taught to do so at school. Her notes confirm the view that civilizations are upheld by schools, that the sense of history is not self-evident but must be inculcated in the individual. Kiseleva is unable to construct her autobiographic narrative so as to make it agree with linear time. Her "individual" time is not the infinite line of progress but rather a system of loci.

Repressions, dekulakization, and prison camps are not mentioned in the notes, with the exception of a concentration camp for Soviet prisoners of war and the Soviet camps for Nazis. Describing the latter, she emphasises that Germans held in imprisonment would be given a daily ration of 1,200 grams of bread – the same quantity that Soviet miners received under the strict rationing system of the time. Life inside the camp fence is not that different from life outside it with respect to the degree of violence and aggression. In fact, there is no demarcation line between them. However, as the earlier quotation concerning the *chernyi voron* (Black Maria – i.e., the car of the KGB) suggests, fear arises easily.

How does Kiseleva enter the wider system of social bonds presented by society at large? She has no confidence whatsoever with respect to the local authorities, whom she knows personally. Power that is close at hand will naturally be unjust. Justice is sought at the hands of distant authorities – incarnated, for example, in the personae of Valentina Tereshkova (i.e., the world's first woman cosmonaut) or Leonid Brezhnev. The "centre" is very far away, but in relation to Kiseleva's "narrow circle" it stands on the periphery. A letter written by Kiseleva on behalf of her grandchildren, which she quotes in the notes, belongs to the discursive type of *chelobitnaia* – a genre of traditional peasant petition.

Having mailed the letter Kiseleva prays: 'I pray to God that Yura (her grandson – N.K.) will be able to stay in the apartment with his family, Lord help us sinners, and I say the Our Father' ('молю бога что-бы Юра из своей симей остался в этой квартире, господи помоги нам грешным, и читаю отченаш') (TsDNA, f. 115, d. 2, 1. 18).

This textual combination of a letter with a fragment of a prayer makes one feel that both of these speech genres – a letter "to the top" and a prayer – perform the common function of appealing to "superior judgement". The writer resorts to a codified language when she seeks an objectification of her utterance. Incidentally, Kiseleva's notes shatter the widely-held belief that the *sovok* (Russian derogatory for a Soviet citizen) is prone to social parasitism. Kiseleva appeals to the state authorities just as she prays to Our Lord for mercy, but she still relies more on her own resources. It is understandable that people should mention Fate when trying to deny a part of their personal responsibility.

The notes give evidence of Kiseleva's attempts to make use of an established rhetorical code (the ideological meta-narrative of the Soviet society). Her effort is naive and awkward. But that is precisely what gives one a sense of the pragmatics of this code. By appealing to the official ideological language ordinary people seek to establish a relation to the general, the universal, and thus to present an argument that is valid for the whole of the society they live in.

Another example: Kiseleva addresses an appeal to a hard-hearted superior:

> Your so Unconsious, your a Party man and hes in the komsomol, if anything happens to the country your in it together youll have to go and figt together, so he got his Consiousness back and asked why didnt he come himself instead of sending his Granny along to do it for him (Какой вы несознательной, вы партейный а он комсомолец если чуть в стране стрясется вы-же вместе, в переди сражатся пойдете, в него пришло сознание спросил, а где он что непришол сам а бабушка за ниво пришла) (TsDNA, f. 115, d. 2, I. 28).

How did it happen that this man 'got his consciousness back'? Did he suddenly have compassion for Kiseleva? Or did the familiar words happen to ring the bell so that he rose at the sound of the trumpet like Tolstoi's 'old regimental horse'? Or perhaps the reason was that Kiseleva's act in citing official discourse not only pointed to the objectivity of her utterance, but also indicated the two speakers' affinity?

As mentioned above, television performed the function of compensating for the loss of a habitual circle of neighbours and relatives. It is through television that political discourse gains access to "consciousness". Kiseleva purchased a TV set late in her life during the time of Brezhnev. This is why she seems to be unaware of Stalin's presence in her past, whereas Brezhnev becomes part and parcel of her life. Unlike that of the Soviet intelligentsia, Kiseleva's attitude toward him was positive. Brezhnev for her is something akin to tsar Alexander III ('the Peacemaker'): 'Im sitting lissning to the radio and there comes the sad news that Lionid I. Brezhnev had died what hartache it braugt me I was seized with fear' ('Слишу по радиво печальную весть умер Брежнев Лионид И. как у меня заболело серце охватил меня страх') (TsDNA, f. 115, d. 2, l. 90).

A link between Brezhnev and Kiseleva is established in so far as official discourse can be re-interpreted in terms of individual life experience.

Conclusions, Or, Rather, Questions

A socio-cultural analysis of Kiseleva's text will, it is hoped, give rise to a discussion of the anthropological and civilizational characteristics of 20th century Russian society.

As suggested in Elias' theory of civilization, the centralisation and monopoly of violence by the state results in highly-developed mechanisms of self-control in people acting on the stage of history. According to Elias, this government monopoly leads to a decrease in individual violence. Thus, violence within society is reduced. To what extent does this hypothesis apply to Soviet society if we take the example of Kiseleva's writing as a part of serial discourse?

The cultivation of self-control as a form of self-repression could be observed in Soviet society but was practised in social spaces, quite different from that described in Kiseleva's notes. Elias' theory could be applied to the Soviet "middle class" in which one could observe an ambition for self-control, a claim for decency, a respect for differentiated codes of conduct, and a definite desire to mark one's own social specificity through "culturedness" *(kul'-turnost')* (Kozlova 1996). But the social space of the Soviet middle class was quite narrow and tight, while the spaces like those described by Kiseleva were, on the contrary, vast. Contrary to Elias' theory the centralised system of violence apparently failed to diminish the extent of individual everyday violence. External social taboos failed to develop into "natural" self-control. The lack of these self-control systems added to the pressure of the centralised violence, from which the mini-community sought escape.

The experience of 20th century Russia, for all its uniqueness, has a universal significance. Several generations have gone through the experience of living more than once on the border of social existence. Famine, cold and the threat of death were not the only hazards. They also had to survive the dissolution of social bonds and the dangers involved in the decline of society into non-society, i.e., into a state where everyone wages war against everyone. Dead bodies were buried without coffins, inedible things had to be eaten. Ontological safety fell to a disastrous level which hindered the cultivation of civilizational qualities. Dangers of this kind are visible in present day Russia. What is more, the past is perpetuated in the present as incorporated history and social memory. Both factors can be seen to play a role in contemporary processes.

A considering 20th century Russia in terms of social existence/non-existence yields new approaches to processes that have so far been discussed only within the framework of socio-political discourse.

Notes

1. The Documentation Centre, *Tsentr dokumentatsii 'Narodnyi Arkhiv'* (TsDNA), is a child of perestroika, an attempt at Russia's first non-governmental archive depository. The initial purpose was to collect rank-and-file sources, testimony left by those who were not prominent in any respect. Thus, unlike state-run archives, this centre would accept whatever document might be deposited. At the current time, *Narodnyi Arkhiv* has many financial problems.

Kiseleva's notes are registered under TsDNA, f. 115. They have recently been published in Kozlova and Sandomirskaya (1996).

References

Barthes, R. (1970) *S/Z*, Seuil, Paris.
Bourdieu, P. (1990) *In Other Words. Essays Towards A Reflexive Sociology*, Stanford Univ. Press, Stanford.
Elias, N. (1978a) *The Civilising Process*, vol. I, Blackwell, Oxford.
Elias, N. (1978b) *What is Sociology*, Cornell Univ. Press, New York.
Elias, N. (1982) *The Civilising Process*, vol. II, Blackwell, Oxford.
Engel'gardt, A. N. (1987) *Iz derevni: 12 pisem. 1872-1887,* Mysl', Moscow.
Gromyko, M. M. (1986) *Traditsionnye formy povedeniia i formy obshcheniia russkikh krest'ian XIX v.*, Nauka, Moscow.
Gromyko, M. M. (1991) *Mir russkoi derevni*, Molodaia Gvardiia, Moscow.
Kotkin, S. (1995) *Magnetic Mountain: Stalinism As A Civilization,* Univ. of California Press, Berkeley and Los Angeles.
Kozlova, N. N. (1996) *Gorizonty povsednevnosti sovetskoi epokhi: golosa iz khora*, Institut filosofii RAN, Moscow.
Kozlova, N. N. and I. Sandomirskaya (1996) *Ia tak tak khochu nazvat' kino. "Naivnoe pis'mo": opyt lingvo-sotsiologicheskogo chteniia,* Gnozis, Moscow.
Rybakovskii, L. L. (1988) *Demograficheskoe razvitie SSSR za 70 let,* Nauka, Moscow.
Scott, J. (1985) *Weapons of the Weak. Everyday Forms of Peasant Resistance,* Yale Univ. Press, New Heaven and London.
Vishnevskii, A. G. (1992) 'Na polputi k gorodskomu obshchestvu', *Chelovek,* no. 1.
Zaionchkovskaia, Zh. A. (1991) *Demograficheskaia situatsiia i rasselenie,* Nauka, Moscow.

The Body and Cultural Transition in Russia

SØREN DAMKJAER

The Lesgaft Academy of Physical Culture in St. Petersburg is situated in the dilapidated buildings of a city mansion of the former tsarist nobility. Founded by the educationalist and reformer Petr Lesgaft, it was, in Soviet times, transformed into one of the elite institutions of Soviet sport and physical culture for the population at large. Like all Soviet institutions of higher education and research, the Lesgaft Academy was deeply affected by the political and economic crisis of the 1990s. But the crisis was not only political and economic. The crisis affected the ideological and educational foundations of sport and physical culture in the post-Soviet order. Indeed, it affected all aspects of body culture and its associated institutions, in post-Soviet society.

In 1994 Jane Fonda, the American movie star and promoter of aerobics for women, was made an official affiliate of the Lesgaft Academy, giving aerobic classes to the Academy's female students. The older generation of professors had regarded aerobics as a kind of sex-gymnastics, totally alien to the moral foundations of the body under socialism. Now, new and more attractive forms of movement had to be introduced to the elite among Russian teachers of physical education. It is not known how Jane Fonda reacted to the low quality of showers, bathrooms and toilets at the Academy. Perhaps, in the manner of Potemkin villages, special facilities were provided for the delicate American female body.

In the rival institution, the All-Russian Academy of Physical Culture in Moscow, aerobics lessons were also introduced, accompanied by wholesale changes in the curriculum of sport and physical education. And, as of 1995, aerobics are being taught in private classes in Vladimir in the former halls of sport societies and factories. But even before the appearance of Jane Fonda in the halls of the Lesgaft Academy, aerobics and shaping were being practiced, in provincial towns as well as the metropolitan centres.

Officers of the All-Russian Ministry of Physical Culture have been thinking up new and attractive ways of providing sport for all. Small groups of youngsters in semi-Russian, semi-American attire are roaming the streets of Moscow and St. Petersburg. Popular magazines of sport are propagating herbal medicine, the Dao of love and sexual happiness. Outside the world of sport, the post-Soviet body of the Russian citizen is entering the world of the consumer society, depending on the availability of economic, cultural and bodily capital. Gone are the days of Soviet puritanism, relative scarcity and uniformity. What we are witnessing is the inauguration of all facets of the post-Soviet body in an unprecedented process of cultural differentiation, eroticisation and distinction. The new models of appearance, fashion and dress are propagated by TV and magazines, emphasising good looks, youth, health, erotic appeal and wealth. The world of culture, too, has discovered the world of the body, ranging from artistic forms of performance to artistic forms of sex show.

Beneath this glittering world of post-Soviet hedonism and consumerism lies the world of poverty, relative destitution, disease and shortened life-expectancies, in short the demografic catastrophe of post-Soviet society. What we are seeing is the construction of a new social body in Russia and the rejection of the concrete bodies of the Soviet past. The new Russian body of the elite mirrors the body of the Western metropolitan centres in New York, Franfurt, Paris and London, but in a kaleidoscopic way. The old Soviet body is being abandoned to oblivion and destitution.

From Unfinished Modernity To Modernity

Following the dissolution of the Soviet Union, Russia is undergoing, or attempting, a transformation from unfinished modernity to modernity or even radical modernity. When applying these terms from the theory of modernisation to the social and cultural changes in the Soviet Union and Russia, one need not refer to some superhistorical and universal model of modernisation. A more cautious sociological theory of modernisation draws attention not only to certain general characteristics of the modernisation process, but equally to the specific cultural forms it takes in a given country and, indeed, to the particular modes of transformation in each case.

This chapter will analyse some of these changes with a special emphasis on certain, often neglected aspects of social life associated with the culture of the body and the fate of the body in the modernisation processes.

The Body In Early Western Modernity

Although classical sociology and most traditional sociology have tended to neglect the body, it has recently aquired status as an object of sociological interest. The body is seen as the effect, cause and sign of modernising processes. The sociology or culturology of the body can briefly be defined as follows: it studies the dimensions of the body, the regimes of the body and all those social and cultural institutions where bodily interaction or bodily signification is important.

A study of modernity must include a study of the institutional processes of differentiation and modes of functioning in institutions of health, consumption, fashion, and sport. Modernisation is not only a question of the differentiation of political and economic systems. Modernity equally requires a number of bodily dispositions, that is, an almost invisible repertoire of bodily and social competences.

The body can be seen as an index of major institutional processes, for instance in institutions of health and disease, sport and recreation, sexuality and reproduction, and consumption. Equally important are systems of representation in which the body figures as an index and icon, as on TV, or in advertising and the performing arts.

Early modernity in Western Europe was characterised by new forms of social institutions of work, family life, consumption and recreation. In general this institutional framework was organised on new patterns of functional differentiation and discipline. In general, old ties of kinship, custom and residence were supplanted by functional ties of class, position in productive organisations, and sport.

In early Western modernity the body in a social context underwent a number of changes. The loosening of social ties and conventions emancipated the body from strict rules of conduct and appearance, making the body a vehicle of individual expression and creation, at least in some sectors of society. The regulation of the body in various institutions such as health, sport, recreation and everyday life was subjected to new functional standards and requirements. The freedom of the body from old social conventions was accompanied by early modern rules of bodily control and appearance. The loosening of external control was counterbalanced by the insistence on internal control and self-management.

Early Russian Modernity

In pre-revolutionary Russia this early modernisation only touched the wealthiests segments of the aristocracy and the small bourgeoisie. Social reforms relating to the health of the urban or rural population were retarded by the cultural and political hegemony of the imperial system and the aristocracy, the crude character of industrialisation, and the poverty of the peasants. Ideas of reform in physical culture and diet were put forward by reformers and leftist groups, but never took root in larger segments of the population.

Surprisingly, however, elements of French fashion spread from Paris to St. Petersburg and even to distant provincial towns in the East and North of Russia. Sorokin observed that items of fashionable dress were introduced in Archangelsk just a year after their introduction in Paris (Sorokin 1994: 198).

Thus, cultural changes did take place place at the turn of the century but these resulted in a mixture of heterogeneous elements of the culture of the body. Periods of hunger among the peasant population were accompanied by visible signs of luxury and fashion in metropolitan and provincial centers.

Early Soviet Reforms

Post-revolutionary Russia in the twenties was characterised by the more or less peaceful coexistence of Russian and international programmes for a rational management of the body. This was broken by the prism of political and cultural movements in the Bolshevik party and other leftist cultural groupings. The context of life reform, sport and health was identical with that of the West, but the cultural context and political influences were different. Obviously, the situation of the population at large restricted these movements to reform the body to small sections of the Party, the intelligentsia etc. The eviction of the aristocracy and bourgeoisie eradicated certain standards of taste in consumption and bodily appearance. The wives of the new party elite, often of humble origin, adopted the tastes of the former upper classes, but virtually lived in a closed "Kremlin prison".

The politics of industrialization were accompanied by a drive to reform dress and physical culture. Here the Soviet management of the body among the masses could be compared to similar tendencies in mass movements in the democratic or fascist west. Common to all of them was the mass, standardised character of gymnastic or sports exercises. The differences between the Soviet Union, Nazi Germany, Italy or the democratic states consisted in the character of the political organisation and the exploitation of the growing interest in physical education and sport among larger groups of society. Mass rallies and sports festivals conducted on the basis of a standardised gymnastic choreography represented techniques for controlling the bodily movements of large groups. These techniques were analogous to the control of bodies in factories, cities and housing complexes.

Thus, modernity invented suitable forms for the control of bodies and these new disciplinary forms of control were designed to erase individual bodily characteristics. These forms required the internalisation of fixed standards of hygiene, movement and diet.

The ideologies of liberalism, socialism and Marxism-Leninism all regarded nature as a battleground for struggle and subjugation, and the bodily nature of man as a battleground for the transformation of the body into an obedient component within the new social order. At the same time, the new sciences of physiology and psychology provided scientific legitimacy for modern methods of bodily control (Eder 1996: 24).

The specific Soviet model of modernisation relied on crude and even cruel methods of control. A remodelling of the behaviour of the population was to be effected through the discipline of the body. The body was seen as a useful instrument for modelling the socialist personality. Standards of bodily perfection were established, and regimes of cleanliness, hard work, obedience and temperance were set up as conditions for the development of a socialist personality. The scientific and ideological ideas in question were derived from biological and sociological reflexolology combined with the ideas of Marxism-Leninism and even progressive ideas from various sources.

The wholesale reorganisation of the system of sport and physical culture from the beginning of the 1930s is to be seen in this context, but it was halted by the Second World War. After the war this centralised system was continued in a situation of relative scarcity. The foundations had been laid for the success of the Soviet elite in international sport. On the whole, however, the Soviet model of modernization remained only a programme. Like many other phenomena in the post-Stalinist era, mass sport was largely a fiction of the planning apparatus, and only small segments among the urban industrial workers, the party apparatus, and the intelligentsia were affected by the appeal for modernising the institutions and regimes of the body.

The Sociology Of The Body

A brief introduction to the key ideas and concepts of the sociology of the body would facilitate our understanding of this type of analysis.

The sociology of the body is a relatively new area of sociological analysis. The key perspective consists in the view that the body is socially and culturally constructed, or rather that the body is the interface of biological, personal, cultural and social orders with a whole array of constructive and deconstructive processes going on. The sociology of the body aims to explain this interrelation between the body and society (Turner 1984).

In order to do so a number of theoretical distinctions have to be made. The first epistemological intervention consists in "dissolving" the idea of the body as an entity. The second consists in introducing "regimes" as intermediate instances between the body and the institutional order. The third intervention consists in analysing all types of social institutions where bodily processes and bodily significations are important.

The Dimensions Of The Body

The body is not regarded as a fixed biological entity but as a complex of dimensions. Some of these dimensions are of a "biological" character, others represent an interface of biological and social constructions, while others are cultural constructions. Examples of the dimensionality of the body are the fundamental dimensions of the inner body, the outer body, the passages of the body, and the surface of the body. Other dimensions of the body consist in volume and height.

The dimensions of the body are ordered in bodily registers. The registers of the senses would be one example. The gaze consists in an ordered and intentional way of looking. Gazing at objects or at other persons is a culturally structured activity of the sense-register of sight. The registers of the senses are an example of the interface of biological and cultural factors. Ways of looking and perceiving represent an interface between cultural categories and the registers of the individual.

The Regimes Of The Body

Regimes constitute the interface between bodily dimensions and social and cultural institutions. Examples of regimes are regimes of movement, regimes of food, regimes of dress, regimes of cleanliness, and regimes of desire. They are, so to speak, the transmission belts between the body and social institutions.

Regimes consist in the concrete rules and regulations of bodily dimensions. The regime of food consists in the rules and regulation for the intake of various natural substances that are subjected to classification and transformation through cooking. Examples of regimes of food could be the diet of a kolkhoz peasant, the diet of the starving population during the years of War Communism, or the diet of prisoners in the Gulag. The regimes of food regulate the growth, size, form and appearance of the body. Ultimately, the regimes of food regulate questions of life and death, as has been evident during Soviet history.

Examples of regimes of movement range from formalised systems of sport and physical culture to patterns of everyday walk and locomotion. These regimes are also culturally structured, contributing to the bodily form of for instance the Soviet ballet dancer, the Soviet elite sportsman or the average Soviet citizen.

Regimes of cleanlines affect all aspects of the dimension of the bodily surface. This regime regulates the removal of bodily waste, from sweat to urine and faeces. It includes the manipulation of bodily passages (mouth, anus) and all secondary "additions" to the surface of the body like cosmetics. This regime removes waste substances and adds new substances to the surface of the body. The regime of cleanliness is practiced in private homes and in public places. In this respect the regime of cleanliness mediates between the private person in the bathroom and the public person in streets and offices.

The processes of modernisation impose strict rules on regimes of cleanliness, cleaning and enclosing the body according to norms of perfection and control of bodily intake, waste and the addition of cosmetics. The Soviet experience is particularly instructive is this respect. Manifestly, the Soviet project had failed in areas of public hygiene. But the rules of bodily cleanliness depended on the cultural and bodily capital of different sections of the population as well. If one looks at the regimes of cleanliness and hygiene, one sees a strange coexistence of public squalor with private cleanliness. The metro systems had no toilets. Public amenities and toilets, with few exceptions, were generally dirty or even filthy. Nevertheless, the standards of cleanliness were maintained in the better off sections of the urban population and standards of high perfection were seen in the female population.

The Institutions Of The Body

A number of social institutions have a particular role in the regulation of the body. These are the institutions of sport, the institution of consumption, the institutions of health and illness, and the institution of desire (sexuality and reproduction). Each institution comprises a number of regimes or articulates the regimes of the body in specific ways.

For instance, the institution of sport obviously articulates the regimes of movement, regimes of food, and regimes of dress. Training and exercise are regimes of movement according to standardised rules concerning the various effects of bodily movement on health, length of life and bodily appearance. Aerobics has a number of standardised exercises to work on particular aspects or dimensions of the body, for instance the metabolism of fat in "fat burning". The regimes of movement in aerobics are also designed to influence the aesthetic and erotic appeal of the female body. In conjunction with regimes of food the exercises of aerobics form the female or male body.

Soviet society developed a number of restricted and standardised forms of movement regimes according to an early modern or modern scheme. This was the essence of Soviet sport and physical culture, and it highlights one important aspect of the Soviet model of unfinished modernity. The differentiation of the institutional structure was never complete. The all-pervading control of Party- and state structures prevented the independence and reflexivity of the institutional order. Sport and physical culture were connected with the work-place. Unions were responsible for mass sport and recreation and, indeed, various aspects of everyday life. Soviet society was, even to the very end, a society of institutional "compactness" and political control.

The institution of consumption regulates the whole world of consumer goods which are in one way or other related to the body. Thus, it unites the institution of production with the regimes of the body. The body moves in cars, eats all kinds of products, cleans itself with all kinds of soap, shampoo, napkins. Each bodily passage has particular products for regulation and cleanlinies from Tampax to electrical toothbrushes. In Soviet society consumption was restricted to a few standardised items which were often deficient in both quantity and quality.

Unfinished Modernity

In using the term "unfinished modernity" to characterise the Soviet Union up to the middle of the eighties, one draws attention to the particular political and cultural forms of Soviet society throughout the Stalin and post-Stalin era. The party-state was an invention to promote modernization from above according to a socialist model of modernity or civilization. The economic model of centralized planning was supposed to organise work and the use of resources according to a rational scheme of production and distribution. A centralised ideological model of cultural values and cultural production in literature, the arts, sport and recreation was supposed to provide the Soviet citizen with a rational and coherent system of cultural values and forms of bodily behavior associated with modernity.

Thus the Soviet model of civilization was quite consistent with the idea of modernity as a plan for a coherent system of social relations and cultural forms that would unite the social individual with the necessary forms of state, economy and culture. In this sense the Soviet model of modernisation as it materialised from the late 1920s and 1930s was deeply functionalist and systematic. The organisation of work, home, sport, and recreation was modelled on the functionalist ideas of early modernity. Standardised activities in physical education, the mass character of sporting events, the incessant propaganda for a communist lifestyle coloured the sports events and the leisure activities of the Soviet citizen. Sport and physical education were seen as instrumental in promoting the model Soviet man and woman as an example of the socialist personality.

The irony of Soviet development consists in the fact that this project of modernity never materialised. Indeed, the Soviet model of modernisation only produced a kind of unfinished modernity. Furthermore, this model of unfinished modernity was unable to change, as became evident during the 1980s.

The reasons for this become clear in a comparative perspective. Modernization in Western Europe, the United States and even Japan did not follow any "total" pattern. The major social and cultural institutions of the economy, politics etc. never coalesced into unified models. Before they became "modern" they changed into something different which sociologists struggle to characterize as postmodern, radically modern or even "risk" societies (Beck 1992).

The Soviet model was able only to create an industrial society within crude forms of political and economic management. It was able only to create cruder forms of discipline and control. The institutions of the body and the regimes of the body were functionalist and politicised, but never internalised except in the institutions of elite sport. It was never able to create the prerequisites for a transition to the much more supple systems of political guidance, personal desires and cultural forms of Western modernity.

The fate of the body in unfinished modernity indicates the failure to programme the institutions and regimes of the body. In principle the Communist project involved a wholesale revolution of bodily institutions and regimes on the basis of a certain concept of the socialist citizen. Forms of hygiene, sport and recreation were therefore central. Furthermore these socialist forms had to be different from bourgeois forms. But in fact, this communist utopia never materialised on a mass scale. The socialist model was able to create an elite system that made the Soviet Union the leading nation in most Olympic sports, but sports for the masses were reduced to a functionalist and restricted form of planned participation which had little appeal to the adult population.

The Transition From Unfinished Modernity To Modernity

The abolition of the Communist Party left the party nomenclature with no political platform, but with new possiblities of manoeuvre. The fragmentation of the party nomenclature into factions involved not only a political struggle but a struggle to convert former political power into economic advantage. What we have seen since the end of the 1980s is an unprecedented struggle on the part of the party nomenclature and related groups to convert political power into personal enrichment and political influence. Since the cultural level of the nomenclature was generally rather low and crude, it is no wonder that the cultural appearance of the "new Russians" involves above all a conspicuous display of wealth.

Cultural Change

Cultural change from unfinished modernity to a post-Soviet form of modernisation is characterised by a movement from duality to multiplicity or even a total dispersion of cultural forms. This applies to bodily institutions and bodily regimes as well. Furthermore, the abolition of the political and cultural hegemony of the Party has obviously led to the disappearance of former distinctions between formal and informal culture.

Among the first elements to disappear was the element of Soviet ceremonial culture. Ceremonial culture can be defined as that form of culture which is associated with public space and public time. 'Public space' in this case means streets and squares, 'public time' anniversaries and holidays. Banners, flags and pictures disappeared within a couple of years, accompanied by the renaming of streets. Statues in metropolitan centres were removed, though they remained in the squares of certain provincial towns. With the disappearence of Soviet ceremonial culture, the new-style Russian holidays consist in the parading of the "new" Russian individual in public places.

The subtle interplay between the dominant culture and oppositional, informal or deviant culture evaporated with the disappearance of the Party and the Union after 1991. The cultural poverty of "official" institutions eroded their dominance, but lack of money meant that the rival "unofficial" institutions and groups did not gain any advantage in the years to come. Cultural institutions had to live on the small state allowances, or on foreign income if possible. This was hardly a situation in which to create new cultural forms from what remained of the peculiarly Soviet perfection of 'bourgeois' cultural forms such as ballet or music. So far the strange political revolutions of 1985 to 1991 have failed to lead to any comparable cultural revolution whatsoever.

Consumer Culture

Soviet society never created a socialist consumer culture. The principles of planned consumption had led to a rationed level of consumption for the majority of the population, who shared the relatively scarce consumer goods according to criteria of political patronage and privilege. Consumer culture remained a particular Western and Japanese cultural institution, based on the availability of consumer commodities which catered for a variety of lifestyles among both the masses and the smaller sections of the population.

The Soviet elites, both the political elite and the intellectual elite, enjoyed certain priviliges of housing, leisure and travel. But these differences in consumption and lifestyle were hardly visible, since the elites enjoyed their consumer privileges in partial secrecy. Moreover, the political elite was in general rather undistinguished in matters of cultural taste.

The first items of Western comsumer culture to appear in the former Soviet Union were popular drinks, like Pepsi Cola, which carried connotations of global culture. A few had been present since the 1970s. Now a host of these products, including McDonald burgers and so forth, was introduced. All were priced to be accessible to almost everyone and carried strong cultural associations with leisure, cheap luxury and America. Simoultaneously, the most expensive and luxurious elements of Western consumer culture, like French perfume and designer clothes and other fashion accessories, began to appear on the scene.

The availability of imported consumer goods quickly led to a sharp differentiation in demand. Those few affluent or extremely rich people who had accumulated wealth from the profitable remnant of the Soviet economy were able to demand a whole range of quality and luxury goods. Western luxury goods defined the taste of these segments. Rarely has the world seen such a display of conspicuous consumption. Whereas Western standards dictate a certain discretion in overtly displaying wealth, such limitations were absent among the new Russians. There was no discreet charm about the new Russian bourgeoisie (see, for instance, the magazine *Elita* 1996).

In other sections of society, especially among the young, access to foreign goods led to a very varied mixture of Soviet and foreign styles in dress, make-up and hair styles. Russian editions of *Cosmopolitan* and *Burda*, or translations of Western books on fashion, makeup, and sexuality presented a variety of models, but for several reasons these models were adopted by young consumers, especially females, in a patchwork fashion.

Fashion And Dress

Regimes of dress and fashion serve in intricate ways to signal cultural differences of gender, age and status. The Soviet model in the last 25 years of its existence showed these cultural processes of differentiation in highly peculiar ways. Items of Western dress to which there was some access in the 1980s carried connotations of youth, fashion and smartness. They were often combined in unexpected ways with elements of Soviet origin.

This tendency was increased in the 1990s when the mass import of "Western" elements of dress began, and that has led to the development of a distinctive Russian "postmodern" style in the cities of St. Petersburg and Moscow, especially as regards the female fashion. Notably, these imports have been grafted on to a long tradition among the female population of investing conspicuously in making themselves pretty and attractive.

What is new, however, is the profusion of Russian translations of books and journals on fashion, home decoration and intimate and sexual relationships. Undoubtedly, much of this literature is a sign of the importation of new lifestyles, but its impact has been largely superficial.

Everyday Life

The social forms of everyday life consist of fluent patterns of bodily and verbal communication and interaction. Everyday life is characterised by the absence of strong and definite social bonds found in the formal institutions of industrial society.

The forms of everyday social interaction in the Soviet period were defined by networks of intimate friends and relations which created a fine web of everyday morality and everyday retreat from the normative and disciplinary modes of official life. There is, however, no reason to romanticise Soviet everyday life, since it involved relatively little by way of material comfort.

Nevertheless, it provided a certain oasis of institutionalised generosity, hospitality, and friendship, and with the changes of the 1990s this oasis came under threat from the increased scarcity of even elementary means for sustaining these cultural standards. This transformation has reduced the level of comfort and security that existed in Soviet times and were a prerequisite for the relative haven of everyday life.

The Individual Body In Post-Soviet Russia

The disappearance of the norms of the State and Party culture, the partial dissolution of the institutional structure of the Soviet model, and the hesitant introduction of new cultural norms have radically and abruptly set the Russian citizen "free". These changes also affect the body. Soviet puritanism has given way to erotic and sexual expression in avant-garde art or pornography. Western models of movement and expression have led to the introduction of fitness and aerobic studios.

In this sense the body of the individual Russian citizen has been emancipated to an unexpected degree. It is naked in a world of change, free to display its new social position and cultural and economic capital in suitable ways. It can do so by combining Soviet and foreign forms of dress, diet and movement without restriction, depending on the individual's economic and cultural capital.

The body of Russian citizen has been emancipated. But the

career of the body has to follow the cultural and economic resources of the individual. Certain social groups such as the aged and the handicapped have been totally dispossessed as elementary provisions have disappeared. Their diet has been reduced to a minimum of bread and tea. Their movement regimes are restricted to the hardships of carrying and walking. Middle groups above the minimum level have lost access to the meagre provisions they enjoyed in Soviet times. Young people are differentiated according to their family's status and connections, their ability to trade etc.

Sport, Leisure And Recreation

The deterioration of living conditions since 1989 has led to a drop in sports participation, which was already low compared to Western Europe and the United States.

Factories and Unions have closed their facilites or hired them out to private entrepreneurs in aerobics. Soon after 1989, the stadiums of the sport clubs or unions began to be used as market places. Activities such as jogging, based on the initiative of individuals or groups of individuals, have hardly gained a foothold in Soviet culture, and attempts to agitate for them in the popular sports magazines have generally been in vain. The new Russian sport organisations have continued using the old moral and political methods, while desperately searching – largely in vain – for a new legitimation for physical exercise.

Lack of facilities and the existential crisis of perhaps two thirds of the population has hardly been conducive to a preoccupation with sport and health. However, small segments of the younger female population in the metropolitan areas or bigger provincial towns have been attracted to expensive private classes in aerobics. Younger Russian women have received new Western models of bodily appearance and appeal and are working hard to meet the standard. Furthermore, the small sections of metropolitan youth wealthy enough to buy roller skates have imitated the skater cultures of Europe and the U.S. On Democracy Day in June 1996 a thousand skaters roamed Moscow in a show of the new fashion. In general, however, only extremely small numbers of young people have taken up these imported and fashionable forms of sport.

Theory And Methodology

Undoubtedly, the Soviet model of unfinished modernisation, and the process of transformation represent a challenge to sociological and culturological analysis. The many forms of analysis current in Europe and the U.S. have not been developed to assess the unexpected changes in the Soviet Union and Russia, but rather to discuss change in Westen modern, radically modern or postmodern societies. The confrontation of these approaches and the comparison with the Soviet Union and Russia represent a challenge, but it is not insurmountable.

The sociology of the body seems to be a profitable approach to a number of questions of cultural change that have been neglected in sociology and cultural analysis. A comparison of various ways of modernising bodily institutions and bodily regimes in Russia, the Soviet Union, post-Soviet Russia, and the West can be instructive in so far as the body is seen as an index and mediator of political and cultural change.

Conclusion

The Soviet model of modernisation succeeded only partially in creating a Soviet body, primarily in elite sport, the army and space flight. Outside these areas, Soviet citizens created all kinds of bodily models, ranging from the suicidal habits of the male population to feminine models of beauty and control.

The transition has set all this in motion, but the direction is not clear. What seems to have followed the transition is a mixture of Soviet and global forms. Jane Fonda may be a passing episode in the history of Russian sport, but it is clear that her appearance is an emblem of the transition from unfinished modernity to a Russian version of modernity and even radical modernity.

In any case the "systemic" transformation following the fall of the Soviet Empire has been accompanied by subtle but equally important cultural changes in everyday life, comsumption, sport and recreation, fashion and festivites. The body is the most visible index of cultural change. What is needed is a systematic sociological approach, such as that suggested by the sociology of the body.

References

Beck, U. (1992) *Risk Society. Towards a New Modernity,* Sage, London.
Eder, K. (1996) *The Social Construction of Nature,* Sage, London.
Turner, B. S. (1984) *The Body and Society,* Blackwell, London.
Sorokin, P. A. C. (1994) *Uchebnik Sotsiologii,* Nauka, Moscow.

National Identity and the Past in Recent Russian Cinema

DAVID GILLESPIE AND NATAL'IA ZHURAVKINA

In the cinema of the Soviet Union, as in its literature, the search for new forms of expression and new ideas of belonging and destiny began in earnest with the death of Stalin in 1953, and assumed certain forms in the 1960s. Particularly since the 1960s writers and film-makers in Russia and the USSR have turned their attention to the historical past in an attempt to find out the truth, and also to reflect on the events and personalities that have shaped the present. This chapter will examine some films of the post-Stalin period that deal with the past in an attempt to give a picture of the emerging notions of national self-awareness and the historical destiny of Russia.

What do we mean by Russian nationalism? In other countries, national identity is framed through the cultural consciousness, political and social institutions and an awareness of the historical forces that have shaped the nation. Russia is a country that before 1 January 1992 had never existed. Before 1917, the Russian Empire embraced many peoples and lands that have since 1991 declared themselves independent, such as Georgia, Ukraine and Armenia. The Russian Federation now stretches from the Baltic to the Pacific, from the Arctic Circle to the sub-tropical reaches of the Caspian, and the search for what it means to be Russian goes on at a time when political institutions have been discredited and the historical past is being rediscovered after decades of falsehood and ignorance. Only the cultural consciousness remains, and this is being constantly enriched and changed as 'new' (in many cases forgotten or repressed) names and works (re-)enter the canon.

Thus, the search for identity is plagued by uncertainties, which themselves give way to extremist positions and polarities (until very recently, the Russian language had no word for 'identity'; now it is a calque: *identichnost'*). For centuries Russia has flirted with the West, the intellectual élite torn between the pull of the Slavophiles, emphasizing Russia's unique standing between Europe and Asia and its consequent moral superiority over the West, and the Westerners, who see Russia as backward and its only path forward through the adoption of Western social-democratic structures and institutions. We find these polarities, and these same parameters, still prevalent in Russian culture, and in particular film, of the past few decades.

Before looking at film, however, it is necessary to discuss ideology. For decades socialist realism was the only acceptable artistic method in Soviet culture, and this method applied equally to music, art, cinema, literature and even architecture. In cinema the screenplay was thus of vital importance, as it was the main means of conveying the propagandistic message. The screenplay would be completed before filming, having been supervised by the Party, and could not subsequently be developed or changed without Party permission. The finished product would then be viewed by Party and film officials.[1] Films which were deemed unsuitable, for whatever reason, were put 'on the shelf' and not made available to the public. Thus in cinema, as in literature, the years 1986-88 largely saw the release of films that had been removed from public circulation, or not made available at all, perhaps for up to twenty years.

Socialist realism also promulgated the idea of the socialist fraternity, the coming together of all peoples under the Soviet banner of internationalism. Individual nationhood was therefore subordinated to the idea of the greater Soviet 'family'. The opening of the floodgates in 1986-87, not surprisingly, saw a release of pent-up anger, frustration and bile that has done much to shape the emerging social and civic consciousness in the Russian cinema. One of the major themes, again not surprisingly, in these years has been the sense of historical injustice, especially crimes committed in the name of the Party under Stalin. The age-old Russian questions are asked: how did this happen? Who is to blame? What are we to do now? What does the future hold? Such questions are at the heart of recent films that confront such seemingly divergent subjects as problems of youth, the investigation of the past, and the soap-opera-like pictures of spiritual and moral conflicts set in a recognizably drab and desolate urban present.

It is instructive at this point to look at the example of literature, as its links with cinema will become increasingly more obvious. There is a clear link between 'village prose' and nationalism in film, for some of the major successes of 'village prose' were made into equally (if not more) successful films. Particular examples here are Elem Klimov's 1983 film *Farewell*, an adaptation of Valentin Rasputin's 1976 novella *Farewell to Matera*, and Vasilii Shukshin's 1973 novella *Snowball Berry Red*, written especially for the cinema and which Shukshin not only directed himself, but in which he also played the leading role. In *Farewell*, a three-hundred-year-old island community on the river Angara in Siberia is threatened with destruction as a hydro-electric dam is built upriver. The dam requires a huge reservoir, of which the river will form part, and, as the water level is to be raised, the village Matera is to be flooded, its culture, traditions and history consigned to oblivion. Both the author of the original novella and the film-maker invest the story-line with considerable lyricism and symbolism, to create an elegy not only for a disappearing rural way of life, but also as a statement on the fate of Russia in the industrial age. There is also considerable anger at the way in which decisions are taken thousands of miles away in Moscow that affect the lives of people whose views are not even sought. In the novella, the bureaucracy, and the so-called 'sanitary engineers' who come to 'cleanse' the island of its trees and houses (so that they do not protrude above the water level after the flooding) are seen in negative, almost inhuman terms, outsiders destroying the homes of others; in the film, the depiction of them is ambivalent, as they are seen as 'necessary'. Vorontsov, their leader, in particular, is portrayed in the film as fired by a vision of the industrialized future, whereas in the novella he is a hack carrying out the orders of others without any thought for the people most directly affected. Both film and novella nevertheless offer an Apocalyptic picture, as Matera is to be razed by fire before being flooded by the rising waters of the dam. Consequently, man's link with the land, and his cherished link with the past and with his ancestors, is lost.[2]

In *Snowball Berry Red* we are introduced to Egor Prokudin, a thief, on his release from prison. He tries to be re-integrated into his former gang, but is soon disillusioned and attempts instead to get a job on a farm and settle down. He goes to live in a village near where he was born. Prokudin, it transpires, was separated from his parents while a teenager, one of the millions of Russians uprooted and torn from their rural origins through the upheavals in the Soviet agricultural community brought about by collectivization in the late 1920s and 1930s. Just as Prokudin appears at last to have found his place – as a tractor driver, symbolically re-establishing his links with the land – his gang come to reclaim him as one of their own, and in the ensuing fight, Prokudin is killed. The film asserts the spiritual superiority of the village over the town, where the village is populated by essentially good and morally wholesome folk, and danger lurks only when outsiders threaten. The town, on the other hand, is the home of criminals and a place of debauchery. Undeniably a powerful and compelling film, *Snowball Berry Red* was phenomenally popular in Russia in the 1970s, testifying to the identification of millions of ordinary Russians, similarly uprooted and alienated, with its central character.

More fundamentally, in both films (as well as the literary works on which they are based), urban lifestyles are consistently contrasted with the lives of simple people from the village. The village and the countryside offer integrity and purity, whereas people from the city have sold their souls in exchange for spurious material benefits. Moreover, the village is the repository of age-old customs and values, it is where the national character itself is rooted. In short, the village is Russia, and the move to urbanization leads to disaster. In the village prose movement, and the films that proceeded from it, there is the affirmation of a mythical picture of Russia, a Russia whose heritage lies in the countryside, and where corruption and ultimately death accompany urban ways and industrialization.

To be sure, the so-called uniquely Russian values of kindness, humility and capacity for honest toil, and the perceived saintliness associated with it, are not the sole preserve of Russian nationalism. Rather, these are the mythical values associated in all societies with living on the land and in harmony with the natural rhythms of life, and part and parcel of what the urban population in industrialized countries would call 'the good old days'. Russian claims to be the custodians of spiritual and moral goodness belie Russia's discomfort with the modern world and its place in it.

Compare this idealization to Andrei Mikhalkov-Konchalovskii's *Asya's Happiness*, a simple and unadorned picture of collective farmers gathering in the harvest over a palpably hot and sweaty summer, and the private life of the Asya of the title. In this film there is no idealization of rural life or the rock-solid values that purportedly emerge from it. Furthermore, there is no cinematic stylization: there is little background music, the action is filmed almost in a documentary, fly-on-the-wall fashion, and there are only two professional actors among the cast. The director allows his villagers to speak in their natural idiom, retelling stories of the War and the Stalinist purges in a natural and straightforward way, without any sensationalism or sentimentality. The overall effect of the film is to give an authentic picture of a strongly bonded community who share the same faith, beliefs and outlook on life, and expect little from life other than what they receive through the fruits of their labour. They are at one with their environment (as the camerawork stresses, catching individuals against the backdrop of fields, river and rolling hills). It is a raw and naturalistic picture, of ordinary people at work and relaxing, speaking about their own lives in their own language, and consciously rejects any nationalist or so-called 'patriotic' interpretation of Russia's hardships. It is perhaps exactly because of the absence of any ideological underpinning that this film was withdrawn from circulation in the USSR for twenty years.

An interesting rejoinder to this film is its sequel, *The Chicken Riaba*, made by Konchalovskii in 1994, in post-Soviet times. Asya is now an alcoholic with a son involved with gangsters, sullen and resentful, as are most in the village, of those few individuals who try to show enterprise and industry in order to better their lives. Villagers actively sabotage the efforts of a local peasant (significantly, a teetotaller) to set up his own business, and carry with them posters of the 1983 Politburo in their desire to return to a communism, or 'democracy', where everyone is poor. They are shamelessly fleeced by gangsters, and turn their aggression on to their own. The film offers a bleak and depressing picture of a demoralized and embittered peasantry, soaked in vodka in the present, and with little sense of a past and no direction in the future. Konchalovskii portrays a Russia of primitive savages united only by their desire to remain savages. These savages are united only in their hatred, and their envy, of those who try to be different, and who are then regarded as enemies.

The films of Andrei Tarkovskii, perhaps the best-known Russian film-maker of his generation, are also relevant here. In such films as *Nostalgia and Sacrifice*, both made in the West, he, too, reflects on Russia's national identity in the form of its relationship with the West. Throughout Tarkovskii's work (and he made only seven films in twenty-five years), the image of the border is predominant, as Tarkovskii's heroes try to define themselves and their country through 'the other'. As so very often in Russian culture, self-definition is attempted not on the basis of what is, but what is not. Whereas in earlier films made in the Soviet Union, such as *Andrei Rublev* and *Mirror*, Tarkovskii had pondered the Russia-West relationship and found scope for cooperation and accommodation between Russia and the West, when he actually arrives and works in the West he rejects any communication. In true Slavophile tradition, a homesick and despondent Tarkovskii sees the West as morally bankrupt and devoid of spirituality, and heading for catastrophe. In *Nostalgia* he rejects the idea of mutual understanding, as he, as *auteur*, tries to transform an Italian landscape into something resembling Russia. Thus, Gorchakov, the central character and Tarkovskii's alter ego, views a mad Italian hermit as a Russian 'holy fool' foretelling the end of the world, and finds it impossible to achieve any real communication with his beautiful Italian guide. She, in particular, is made to look superficial, a Russian speaker who cannot penetrate beyond the surface meaning of the words in the poems she reads (significantly, poems written by Tarkovskii's own father). The end of the film sees the gradual merging of a Russian and Italian landscape, with Russian folk music blending with Verdi's *Requiem* in the background. External landscapes are confused, juxtaposed, but inner, psychological landscapes remain distinct, separate. In *Sacrifice* Tarkovskii's predicted catastrophe happens, as nothing less than nuclear war is the theme.[3]

In this context it is instructive to turn to a documentary film, *The Russia We Have Lost*, by Stanislav Govorukhin. This film offers a kind of socialist realism in reverse, where the Tsarist past and in particular the Tsarist family are presented in glowing colours, with hardly a mention of the repression, poverty, institutionalized antisemitism or chronic civic backwardness historians tell us were prevalent. The destruction of the monarchy is seen here as an unmitigated catastrophe for Russia. Furthermore, the director, who also narrates and presents the film, is intent to impress upon the viewer not only a nostalgic and rose-tinted picture of Russia as a nation with a glorious heritage, but also as a great power. Throughout the film the point of reference is 1913, the year before the outbreak of the First World War, which itself led to the abdication of the Tsar and the Bolshevik seizure of power in 1917. Although Govorukhin admits the personal weakness of the Tsar, he is enamoured of the pageantry and majesty of the royal family, its links with European monarchs, and spares us no details in his blow-by-blow account of the brutal murder and disposal of the bodies of the entire Romanov family in 1918. Significantly, the major circumstance that destroyed the credibility and legitimacy of the Romanov dynasty – the influence of Grigorii Rasputin at court in the last years of the monarchy – is totally ignored in this film.

Govorukhin is also at pains to paint a black picture of Lenin as a cynical opportunist with a pathological hatred of the monarchy, and spends considerable time exploring Lenin's alleged Jewish ancestry. All in all, the glorification of the Tsarist past is not that far removed from the idealization of a mythical Russian Eden in the films of Klimov and Shukshin, and it is not surprising, therefore, that in the closing credits Govorukhin acknowledges in particular his debt to the writings of Alexander Solzhenitsyn. Solzhenitsyn, too, has much in common with the 'village prose' movement – indeed, with his novella *Matryona's Home* in 1963, he started it. The film *The Russia We Have Lost* follows exactly Solzhenitsyn's interpretation of Russian history in the early years of this century, including his advocacy of Stolypin, the reformist Tsarist minister whose efforts to modernize agriculture and the rural community are seen by Solzhenitsyn as offering the way forward for Russia in the years before the First World War. Stolypin was assassinated in 1911, and with him, according to the Solzhenitsyn/Govorukhin variant, went Russia's chances of averting revolution and catastrophe.

The reappraisal of the more recent past, especially the Stalin years, is the most important aspect of the search for identity and justice in post-glasnost' cinema. For these directors, just like writers and journalists, are interested not in the sufferings of the Russian soul, the idea that to be Russian is to 'feel' Russia and be sensitive to the Russian soul, but rather concentrate on actual facts, events and personalities. The first major film to explore the impact of Stalin's terror on family life was not a Russian film at all. The Georgian Tengiz Abuladze's 1987 film *Repentance*, through a mixture of religious symbolism, allegory and fantasy, offers a relentless picture of the destruction of a family in a police state run by a ruthless dictator, Varlam. But more fundamentally, the dictator's own family are unable to live down the consequences of his tyranny. After his death Varlam's grandson commits suicide.[4] The relationship of the individual to tyranny has also been explored in *The Servant*, made in 1988 by Alexander Mindadze and Vadim Abdrashitov (also non-Russians). Here the relationship of two men, one an important official, the other his driver, is turned into an allegory of power and submission. It is not so much the official who imposes his will on his driver (and others); rather the driver has an inner need to be subservient. Thus, too, the Russian people were tyrannized for a quarter of a century because they wished to be tyrannized. (Many in Russia today, of course, still yearn for the 'iron hand' of a strong leader to restore 'order'.)

Mark Zakharov's film *To Kill A Dragon* is in many ways similar, for although the tyrant, in the shape of a dragon, is killed repeatedly, it keeps re-appearing in different guises, and the end of the film suggests that the dragon exists inside all of us and will never be thoroughly destroyed. The theme of tyranny is explored also in Iurii Mamin's film *Sideburns*. Here a group of young men, devotees of Pushkin, terrorize a local community through demagogy by insisiting on adherence to what they see as pure Russian values, as symbolized in the poetry of Pushkin. The sideburns they wear in deference to their master serve as the symbol of their nationalistic despotism. Mamin thus subverts the chauvinistic ethos of those in Russia who call for an 'ethnic cleansing' of today's culture.

Tarkovskii's film *Stalker* can also be mentioned in this respect, for the Stalker of the title guides a curious writer and professor around the 'zone', an area placed off-limits by the authorities and guarded by sentry posts, barbed wire and machine-gun toting guards. These representatives of the modern, urban intelligentsia (symbolizing respectively the heart and the mind, the soul and the intellect), are looking for some truth and meaning to their lives, and require an outstanding individual to guide them to it. Is there any essential difference here between the tyrant-figures of Mamin, Zakharov, Abuladze and Mindadze and Abdrashitov, and Tarkovskii's bewildered individual who claims spiritual and moral superiority over his cynical, world-weary charges? All of these films are united by their fascination with the figure of the leader, the individual who craves control over the lives of others.

The exploration of the Stalinist terror has perhaps reached its apogee in Nikita Mikhalkov's film *Burnt By The Sun*, released in Russia in late 1994. Enormously succesful both in Russia and abroad, it tells the story of Divisional Commander Sergei Kotov, hero of the Revolution and Civil War, arrested by the NKVD in the summer of 1936 and subsequently shot. He is arrested by Mitia, formerly with the Whites who bought his way back into the Soviet Union, and into the NKVD, by betraying leading members of the White emigration. The picture we get of Russia before the storm is of a calm, ordered dacha lifestyle, where characters drink tea, converse, play, argue and make love. Both the leading characters, the representatives of the dying order and the victors respectively, are contrasted throughout. Kotov is a man of the people, a Russian who prefers to wash in the old rustic bath-house rather than in a modern bathroom, and who speaks in the language of the foot soldier. Mitia is educated and well versed in Western culture. It is a powerful film about the death of a generation, but it is also about the assault on Russia by non-Russians. *Burnt By The Sun* is neo-Slavophile in its portrayal of the destruction of real Russian values, but it obviously also has much in common with *Repentance*.

Another film that looks back to the 1930s is Aleksei German's *My Friend Ivan Lapshin* (1985), a film based on the literary works of Iurii German, the director's father. The plot deals with the local policeman, Lapshin, and his eventual tracking down of a local band of violent criminals, but the film also evokes the atmosphere of provincial Russian life in the 1930s, when the action is set. There is no explicit mention of the historical background, such as collectivization, purges, mass starvation in the countryside (save for a portrait of Stalin glimpsed towards the end of the film), but the ordinary life of people is portrayed as hard and sometimes brutal. Here people live together in communal apartments, have little or no privacy, and criminals are shot in cold blood by the police. With its candid portrayal of life in 1935, the film undoubtedly has a nostalgic appeal for many Russians, but on a deeper level the director is subverting the socialist realist depiction of reality that his father gives in his stories. Set just before the onset of the Great Terror, the film offers hints at what is to come. Furthermore, the film's plot is narrated retrospectively, thus establishing a broad temporal perspective. Thus, the times live on in the present through the memory of the narrator.[5]

In the 1970s and 1980s there have been several popular and respected films dealing with life in Russia before the Revolution. What is of interest in these films is the absence of any explicit ideology condemning the iniquities of that time. Moreover, films based on works by classical Russian authors, such as *Unfinished Piece for Mechanical Piano*, directed by Nikita Mikhalkov in 1976, *Vassa*, directed by Gleb Panfilov in 1983, and *Cruel Romance*, directed by El'dar Riazanov in 1984, are based, respectively, on pre-revolutionary literary works by Anton Chekhov, Maksim Gor'kii and Alexander Ostrovskii (to be sure, Gor'kii rewrote his play *Vassa Zheleznova* in the 1930s). Each of the directors displays a deep reverence for the literary source, both in characterization and fidelity to the original plotline, but each film has a contemporary resonance. Mikhalkov's film, in particular, is purportedly about the inner torments and self-doubt of a failed radical at the turn of the century, but it also contains many passages that can be interpreted as an explicit comment on the capitulation of the Soviet intelligentsia in the 1970s. In all of these films it is as if the problems of collective and individual morality, emotional vacuity and spiritual malaise, prevalent in Tsarist society, are equally true of the modern age. Individual morality is measured against the touchstone of Russian literature of the nineteenth century. These film-makers demonstrate above all a cultural continuity between past and present.

In a different context one of the key films of the 1970s is *The Garage,* directed in 1979 by El'dar Riazanov, with a script by himself and Emil' Braginskii. It is a satire, a genre very difficult to practice in Brezhnev's Russia, and its target is the selfish materialism of modern Muscovites. The plot revolves around a meeting called in a research institute to decide who is to lose their allocated garage space because of a planned motorway route. In fact, the institute's leadership has already decided on the four people who will lose out, and the meeting is intended merely as a rubber stamp exercise. However, in the course of the evening – and then the night and the following morning, as those present are locked in – not only are the greedy and self-serving instincts of today's intelligentsia laid bare, in varying degrees, but the collective overturns the decisions laid down from on high and asserts its own priorities. Those who lose out, in the end, are the highly-connected and those in positions of power, and a new order is born. Amid chaos and anarchy (some of it extremely funny), the old élite is overthrown. Thus the film can be seen as an allegory, and a remarkably perceptive and prophetic one, about the revolt of the masses against their leaders, and the overthrow of the social hierarchy. At the end of the film, the last garage space to be lost is decided by drawing lots. In other words, democracy replaces autocracy. It is remarkable that this film was allowed to appear in Brezhnev's time, for it offers a subversive picture of what can be achieved with 'people power'. The world was to be witness to a much greater illustration of this in 1991.

Russians today grope their way towards an as yet uncertain identity, an unknown destiny. This is an identity not as yet based, as in Western Europe, on political institutions, but above all on culture, and the cultural consciousness is one which 1917 did not break. Russian culture has always been deeply religious, and it is perhaps worth pointing out here some films with a clear Christian subtext. Larisa Shepit'ko's war film *The Ascent*, made in 1976, offers a picture of a Soviet partisan tortured and eventually executed by the Germans, and whose death scene is framed in hallowed light as he assumes a Christ-like aura. *Scarecrow*, directed in 1987 by Rolan Bykov, is the story of the persecution of a girl by her classmates, and her suffering is increasingly seen as a martyrdom.[6]

To conclude: in the years since Gorbachev came to power and effectively ushered in the end of totalitarianism, national identity has come to be based on the national experience, harrowing though this has been, and the people's culture. Given the cataclysms of twentieth century Russian history, the assault on its culture by Bolshevik ideology, and the decimation of its people, it is no wonder that the current search for identity and purpose is beset by bitter argument and division. One of the themes that unite such otherwise disparate films as *The Russia We Have Lost* and *The Chicken Riaba* is the sense of hatred for a perceived enemy, for 'the other'. For some national identity becomes associated with a glorification of the past, the assertion of a mythic, golden age of order, stability and above all faith in the destiny of Russia. On the other hand, there are film-makers intent on exploring the actual events and experiences of the past in order to convince people of the evil of totalitarianism, to avoid a repeat of past mistakes in the future. The exorcism of the past and the search for new meanings and forms continues apace. Above all, these strivings offer direction and a sense of purpose for the future.[7]

Notes

1. For a concise and illuminating account of socialist realism in Soviet film, and the stranglehold the Party managed to exert on film production under Stalin, see Peter Kenez, *Cinema and Soviet Society*, 1917-1953, Cambridge Univesity Press, 1992, especially pp. 101-85.

2. The most comprehensive account of Russian village prose can be found in Kathleen Parthé, *Russian Village Prose: The Radiant Past*, Princeton University Press, 1992.
3. I have written at more length on Tarkovskii's neo-Slavophilism in my paper 'Russia and the West in the Films of Andrey Tarkovsky', *New Zealand Slavonic Journal*, 1993, pp. 49-61.
4. For a full discussion of this important Soviet film, see Elizabeth Walters, 'The Politics of Repentance: History, Nationalism and Tengiz Abuladze', *Australian Slavonic and East European Studies*, vol. 2, no. 1 (1988), pp. 113-42.
5. For a fuller discussion of this film, see Benjamin Rifkin, 'The Reinterpretation of History in German's Film *My Friend Ivan Lapshin*: Shifts in Center and Periphery', *Slavic Review*, vol. 51, no. 3 (Autumn 1992), pp. 431-47.
6. For a fuller discussion of this film, see Benjamin Rifkin, 'The Christian Subtext in Bykov's *Chuchelo*', *Slavonic and East European Journal*, vol. 37, no. 2 (Summer 1993), pp. 178-93.
7. For further discussion of cinema in Russia today, see the following: Anna Lawton, *Kinoglasnost: Soviet Cinema in Our Time*, Cambridge University Press, 1992; Andrew Horton and Michael Brashinsky, *The Zero Hour: Glasnost and Soviet Cinema in Transition*, Princeton University Press, 1992; Julian Graffy, 'Unshelving Stalin: After the Period of Stagnation', in Richard Taylor and Derek Spring (eds), *Stalinism and Soviet Cinema*, Routledge, London and New York, 1993, pp. 212-27.

Filmography

Asino schast'e (Asya's Happiness), dir. Andrei Mikhalkov-Konchalovskii, 1967.
Bakenbardy (Sideburns), dir. Iurii Mamin, 1990.
Vassa (Vassa), dir. Gleb Panfilov, 1981.
Voskhozhdenie (The Ascent), dir. Larisa Shepit'ko, 1976.
Garazh (The Garage), dir. El'dar Riazanov, 1979.
Zhestokii romans (A Cruel Romance), dir. El'dar Riazanov, 1984.
Zerkalo (Mirror), dir. Andrei Tarkovskii, 1975.
Kalina krasnaia (Snowball Berry Red), dir. Vasilii Shukshin, 1973.
Kurochka Riaba (The Chicken Riaba), dir. Andrei Mikhalkov-Konchalovskii, 1994.
Moi drug Ivan Lapshin (My Friend Ivan Lapshin), dir. Alexei German, 1985.
Neokonchennaia p'esa dlia mekhanicheskogo pianino (Unfinished Song for Mechanical Piano), dir. Nikita Mikhalkov, 1976.

Nostal'giia (Nostalgia), dir. Andrei Tarkovskii, 1983.
Offret (Sacrifice), dir. Andrei Tarkovskii, 1986.
Pokaianie (Repentance), dir. Tengiz Abuladze, 1987.
Proshchanie (Farewell), dir. Elem Klimov, 1983.
Rossiia, kotoruiu my poteriali (The Russia We Have Lost), dir. Stanislav Govorukhin, 1992.
Sluga (The Servant), dir. Vadim Abdrashitov, screenplay by Alexander Mindadze, 1988.
Stalker (The Stalker), dir. Andrei Tarkovskii, 1979.
Ubit' drakona (To Kill A Dragon), dir. Mark Zakharov, 1988.
Utomlennye solntsem (Burnt By The Sun), dir. Nikita Mikhalkov, 1994.
Chuchelo (Scarecrow), dir. Rolan Bykov, 1987.

The Individual and the Collective: A Cultural Approach to the Question of Dualism in Soviet Society

Hans Henrik Brockdorff

In this chapter I shall concentrate on the problem of the individual and the collective in Soviet society and shall examine some traits of dualism in this context. I will be focusing on manifestations which diverge from the official collectivistic outlook and which enable us to gain insight into ideas and trends, existing behind the facade. I find it appropriate to base this examination on material whose significance and relevance can be seen by the status it acquired in the cultural context as soon as the straitjacket of ideology was loosened at the end of the 1980s. Concretely, I will look at the alternative, formerly disdained philosophical heritage that underwent a revival (or was legitimised) on the threshold of the 1990s and at aspects of the underground culture, sometimes also known as the 'second culture' *(vtoraia kul'tura)* as opposed to official culture. Finally, I will discuss some of the implications involved in the overcoming of the old 'master-slave' structure and the shaping of a new cultural formation.

This study thus contains the following elements: 1) an explication of ideas differing from Soviet-Marxist ideology 2) an examination of underground culture as a straightforward, uncensored expression of moods otherwise modified in officially-accepted culture and 3) a look at the new context, where different aspects of culture can coexist freely. This point leads to a question about the substance of the new, complex cultural pattern. Complexity is the sum of different parts, including discordant parts which may reflect former dissonances or show new variations on the theme of dualism. To illustrate the subject as clearly as possible, I will focus on texts which in some way intercommunicate (the problem in one text reflecting the problems in another), in the belief that this qualitative approach reveals certain essential aspects of Soviet/Russian culture. I should add that in so far as culture can be said to consist of 'patterns, explicit and implicit, of and for behaviour acquired and transmitted by symbols, constituting the distinctive achievement of human groups, including their embodiment in artifacts' (Kroeber & Kluckhohn 1952: 181), I find it relevant to attach some symbolic values to the material too. But before we go more closely into the material itself, some common remarks must be made.

The Dichotomy in Soviet Life

Soviet society can in many ways be seen as a dichotomic society, consisting of two layers, the official normative level, and an underlying layer. This applies not least to culture and consciousness. It finds its ultimate form in the 'classic' Soviet society of the 1930s, with its well-known enthusiasm on the one hand, and its suppressions and prohibitions on the other. In its subsequent evolution it would follow the same model in a modified form. As far as the individual is concerned, it means a recognition, or acceptance, of Soviet reality, combined with a more or less conscious awareness of personal discomfort and lack of integrity. The use of the term 'enthusiasm' may of course be disputed. Moreover one should be cautious about dividing the 'two layers' too strictly: they are intertwined as well.[1] But in an examination of culture and consciousness in the Soviet society it is none the less essential to operate with this two-level structure.

The vacuum resulting from the disappearance of a previously fixed point of reference in the second half of the 1980s intensified the search for alternatives. In this context – as evidence of the relevance of the formerly neglected personal, individual layer – the focus shifted especially to texts which reflected the contradictions of Soviet/Russian society and which emphasised the needs of the individual.

Society and the Individual in the Interpretation of Formerly Disregarded Philosophers

I will briefly mention some of the thinkers who are now receiving renewed recognition. One such is N. Berdiaev, advocate of the personality doctrine. Instead of the old Cartesian dualism of soul and body, spirit and matter, he spoke of the dualism of spirit and nature, freedom and necessity, persons and things. The human body, even 'the body' of the world, can leave the 'sphere of nature', of 'necessity' and 'things' and pass into the sphere of 'spirit,' of 'freedom', of 'personality' (Berdiaev 1965: 164-5). According to Berdiaev, the mistake of Communism lay in its belief in the possibility of realising human brotherhood by compulsion. But Communism in some way did fit in with the Russian mind, Berdiaev claims. In fact, an eschatological element, the feeling of an end goal, has always been present in Russian thought, though it might in some cases take on a religious or materialistic colouring. This is connected with the historical conditions of Russia. The famous schism *(raskol)* entailed a voluntary self-exclusion from history, based on the conviction that the Lord of this world ruled over history, the Anti-Christ, who had seized the church and the state. Religion, the Orthodox faith, was forced to go underground. The real kingdom was the mythical town of Kitezh, situated somewhere at the bottom of the sea. The 'left wing' among the Old Believers was apocalyptic in character.

Similarly, the Russian intelligentsia (in the 19th century) tried to escape the painful realities of Russian life by means of an ideal reality. This ideal reality might be pre-Petrine Russia, the West or the prospect of revolution. The failure of the Church to satisfy the spiritual demands of the population because of its servile attitude towards the state threw the people into the hands of the Bolsheviks, who took advantage of their propensity for symbols and myths. In fact, there was a reverse religiosity in the orthodox maximalism of Bolshevism. Berdiaev makes the subtle observation that: 'The main thing in the Russian revolution was not the proletariat, but the idea of the proletariat, the myth of the proletariat' (Berdiaev 1990, 2: 151). There are many such precise observations and subtle aphorisms in Berdiaev's writings on the nature of the revolution and Russian society. At the same time one may be troubled by his consequent emphasis on the irrational forces that determine history, an emphasis which makes it hard to see the overcoming of restrictions and the realisation of the individual in something other than non-earthly terms.

A more simple, but no less interesting interpretation of the contradictions inherent in Russian life was offered by Evgenii Trubetskoi. In an article written in 1906 (shortly after the February revolution and the dissolution of the newly-established Duma) he indicated the two possible directions in which Russian society, in his opinion, might evolve. One would assert the principle of equality in terms of the power of the people, and would be tantamount to the suppression of freedom, censorship and the denial of the rights of the individual (entailing full dependence on the judgements of the majority *(bol'shinstvo)*). The other would be based on an understanding of the ethical foundation of civic society, that is, on respect for the individual as the guarantee of personal freedom, regardless of whether that individual belongs to the majority or minority. Either there would be a general levelling, in other words, or a more nuanced society. Accordingly, he in part associates the principles of the democratic election system, 'universal, direct, secret and equal' (hence the title of the article: 'Vseobshchee, priamoe, tainoe i ravnoe') with a symbol of levelling, the cemetery – the 'classic expression of universality, equality and the secret of death, the direct destiny in store for all of us' – and in part with a promising building on the ground, a church, rising on the Russian plain, as an 'ideal of positive universality and equality, since in Christ there is no difference between the Hebrew and the Hellene, nor between the slave and the master, it is an expression of the highest secret in human existence, the direct way to salvation' (Trubetskoi 1990: 200). In plain words, he stresses the importance of diversity as opposed to uniformity, of democracy instead of totalitarianism. By the same logic, he likewise rejects the idea of a specific Russian Messianism (concretely, his criticism was addressed to Sergei Bulgakov and Berdiaev, each of whom offered an interpretation of this idea). Instead of claiming the uniqueness of any given nationality – which, in his view, entailed the elevation of the limited into norm and ideal

– he argues, without neglecting specific cultural traits, for the inclusion of the specific into the entirety. National values, single rays of light, should not be isolated; they are part of the spectrum that constitutes the unity of sunlight. This notion likewise determines Trubetskoi's aesthetics. Culture is seen as openness and dialogue. If icon painting flourished in the Novgorod republic, the Russian Florence, it declined after the fall of Novgorod because of its elevation into an art representing autocracy in the studios of the Moscow Kremlin in the 17th century (Trubetskoi 1990: 212, 221). Thus, Trubetskoi sees the vitality of culture in the interaction of cultures.

Another thinker who is relevant in this context is Simon Frank. Domiciled in Western Europe after being exiled from Russia in 1922, he sought to formulate specific as well as common traits concerning the conditions of human existence, and to define the disavowed identity of his own cultural starting-point by comparing it to what he felt was the essense of self-understanding in the world he was confronted with now. His own situation lent a special intensity to the problem of the individual's sphere of action in a world that was tilting towards totalitarianism. Rejecting Soviet-Marxist determinism, he seeks to define the individual within his surrounding context, and in outlining the specific traits of his own culture he includes characteristics prevailing in Western thought. From Descartes onwards, Western philosophy, he argued, had been focusing on the 'Ego', the subject, markedly reducing the role of the object (the others, the outer world were assigned a secondary role in the perception of the subject, or the possibility of such perception was even denied), but a definition of the 'I' need not necessarily be tied to this subject-fixation. Frank undertakes a linguistic, morphological analysis of the substance of the 'I'. The 'I' attains its distinctiveness in relation to 'you'; it would be impossible to determine its specificity without this comparison. The latter is the prerequisite for speaking about the former. Thus, rather than being opposed, 'you' and 'I' depend on one another. This reciprocal relationship becomes even clearer when we look at the plural form. 'We' not only means a multitude of different 'I's, but above all the connection of a single person (the one who speaks or writes the word 'we') with some other persons (one or more of 'you'). In Russian this correlation gets even more stressed in the specific plural/dual form *my s toboi (my s nei, my s nim, my s vami* etc.) which clearly underlines the relation of the 'I' with somebody else. *My s toboi* (you and I) can agree or disagree *(my s toboi soglasny/nesoglasny)*, but this does not change anything in the correlation given in the complex pronoun. In this sense, any personal statement also depends on a context. The point is that the 'I' is seen as part of the whole; the distinctive features appear against this background. And in this subject-object-relation (which he elaborates in his book *The Spiritual Foundations of Society*, 1930) Frank sees the essential traits in the apprehension of the 'I' and its correlates which he characterises with the term *sobornost'* ('communion').[2] The possibility of a dialogue within his native country was, as I have mentioned, interrupted for Frank himself in 1922. But with perestroika his ideas of the individual and the community have acquired fresh relevance with regard to the creation of a pluralistic society. *'My s nim/s nei'*, understood both as an entirety and as the sum of the components forming it, on the basis of interaction, could be seen as a formula of discussion within a frame of consensus (as opposed to the uniforming *'my '* used by Zamiatin in the title of his anti-Utopian novel from the 1920s). The degree to which the *'my s nim '*-principle has been fulfilled could be regarded as one measure of the extent to which pluralism had been achieved or implemented.

Frank's definition of the 'I' and its context is in fact quite modern. One might in this connection reflect on his use of the term *sobornost'*. When Frank uses this predicate with reference to his subject-object-relation, it is partly in order to call attention to a disdained tradition, but, probably, too, because he did not find such a correlation in contemporary Western Europe. (In Germany he found himself an object of persecution by the Nazis and left the country in 1937; thereafter he lived in Paris and died in London in 1950.) His *sobornost'* refers to a national tradition, but is not equivalent to narrowness. As he puts it in another work: 'The finite is that which does not contain the fullness and is therefore only a part; the finite is that which has limits, and limit is a line of demarcation between "one" and "the other"' (Frank 1965: 293). Continuing the Frankian use of pronouns we could say that *'my s nimi'* (they and us) would indicate a hope of positive interrelations on earth. Frank himself, confronted with a chaotic world, pointed to the importance of ethics, the personal responsibility of creating some kind of light through one's actions in a time of darkness.

The Underground. Stages on its Road to Recognition

This philosophical heritage became a visible part of the cultural context at the end of the 1980s. This does not mean that it was unknown in the years before. But, like other manifestations of alternative culture, it had to vegetate in isolation. In the wake of the Thaw, and the expectations it raised, various facets of culture had to go underground. In the underground we find an interest in the national heritage as well as in Western culture. The individual had become isolated. The impossibility of dialogue meant that certain authors felt the need to place themselves as the principal characters in works of fiction. In this respect one notable example of the 'other culture' *(vtoraia kul'tura)* is the novel *Moscow-Petushki* (1969) by Venedikt Erofeev. The 'hero' of the novel is Venia Erofeev. The author knew that his novel was unlikely to be published, and therefore wrote without any concern for convention. His language differs markedly from the normative language of the state, as does his use of symbols; in fact, the whole novel is antithetically structured to contrast with official values. The 'hero' has a deepfelt aversion towards the symbolic (as well as concrete) centre of Soviet power, the Kremlin in Moscow; he avoids it when walking around in the streets of Moscow and even insists that he has never seen it. Accordingly, his lodestar is not the red star above the Kremlin, but the star of Bethlehem. Hence the narrative itself is formed as a movement away from Moscow, to some paradisaically imagined Petushki. But he never gets there. In fact, in the end he finds himself back in Moscow, and not only somewhere in Moscow, but up against the Kremlin wall, hunted by four apocalyptical figures. His attempts to escape are in vain. Despite all allusions to the Testament there is no salvation, no resurrection, for Venia Erofeev. He is just a human being, caught up in a totalitarian society. His last words, after he has been tortured by the militiamen, thus read as follows: 'Then I lost consciousness, and have never regained it' (Erofeev 1977: 73). In a society dominated by class consciousness, the only thing for a decent person to do seemed to be to black out.

Of course, alternative manifestations were not only present in underground and dissident culture. Alternatives to the official outlook were articulated in official, or 'permitted' culture as well. But any person involved in culture had a well-developed sense of where the line of demarcation was. Step over this invisible line, and you were lost.

I had a friend who worked at the publishing office of the church, and as secretary to one of the metropolitans. His name was Vladimir Rusak and he lived in an apartment in the outskirts of Moscow. I had not seen him for a couple of years, and wanted to get in touch with him. I could not find him. I even went to his former working place at the Novodevichi monastery. They could not help me. Wherever I asked, I was given the same vague answers. He might be in Minsk, I was told. I could have gone to Belorussia, but as it turned out there was no reason for me to do so. Vladimir Rusak had, indeed, been in Vitebsk for a while and had delivered a sermon in the Kazan' church in March 1982, speaking about people's neglect of their ancestral roots. 'We have forgotten about our ancestors' pains and sufferings, we have criminally lied about their deeds,' he said. 'Instead of pointing at those who were guilty of their martyrdom, we have casuistically put the blame on the martyrs themselves' (D'iakon 1986: 32). After this he lost his job, and, like many other intellectuals – those depicted, for instance, in Sergei Kaledin's *The Humble Cemetery* – was forced to earn his living through odd jobs. But the situation got even worse, for in 1986 he was arrested. He had completed a study of the history of the Church, and had incautiously shown it to his spiritual superiors.

So if there were no dialogues, there were many interesting monologues. The artist Il'ia Kabakov has sought in his *Memoirs* to capture the characteristics of this underlying cultural layer. He describes, how the underground artist would try to reach out for vital elements that existed outside the stifling, oppressive world around him, whose breath on the back of his neck the artist felt constantly. He was like a person sitting underwater who attempts to breathe through a reed, or who jumps to catch a glimpse of what lies above the surface. His discoveries might therefore be somewhat fragmentary. Yet what mattered was the attempt to bridge the abyss and seek inspiration in styles and tendencies which could satisfy the artist's own demands (Kabakov 1990: 6)[3], be these suprematism, Russian art of the twenties, surrealism, fauvism or whatever. 'Elements of a classic model of democratic culture,' as one art critic puts it, 'became prerogatives of individual artistic standpoints' (Erofeev 1988: 45). From the outset, moreover, there were certain common traits in this unofficial art. It had, for instance, a certain irrational, metaphysical character. The surrounding world, if it appeared in the work of art, was mostly reproduced in caricature, as in the paintings of Sitnikov, where stylised churches with crosses and onion cupolas are surrounded by drunkards and cripples. At the same time there was a prevalent tone in these works of art: a prevailing whiteness. White is associated with eternity and harmony, and the artist may try to create this sense of whiteness through contrasting elements. Kabakov speaks of the 'metaphysics of white', for instance, in the work of Erik Steinberg in the 1960s and the first half of the 1970s (Kabakov 1990: 7). An exhibition of this artist's work took place in Copenhagen in 1993.

But we can also see another tendency in the unofficial art that began to emerge in the 1970s. It expresses above all the tension arising from an unresolved discrepancy between art and reality, and between the position of the individual and society. This 'social art' – manifested, for example, in 'soc-art' and 'concept-art' – no longer turns away from Soviet reality, but seeks to challenge it. The sense of discrepancy (between the postulated autonomy of the creative artist and his concrete existence in the Soviet society), was exacerbated by the fact that official propaganda had become more and more hollow, platitudinous and routine. Thus the artist sought to challenge official imagery and language in an attempt to overcome them. Soc-art and concept-art accordingly work with stereotypes of everyday Soviet life (posters, slogans, newspaper texts), 'activising' the clichés involved, extracting new connotations from them, and thereby distancing them as objects of reflection. This new approach is well expressed by Lev Rubinstein, who says that concept-art represents more a relationship to style rather than a style in itself, in so far as it means that 'a text can be an object of analysis, while at the same time objects can be seen as texts' (Rubinstein 1990: 47). Behind efforts like these lies a desire for emancipation from the material. As Dmitrii Prigov puts it:

> Only by entering the zone of this language (without cursing it or pretending that it does not exist) will one be able to understand it in oneself, in all of us <...> By realising this, by reflecting on it and talking about it we can achieve a new metaplane for manipulating the signs of this language, which, when transferred to the sociocultural and sociological sphere, gives a new layer of understanding and freedom (Prigov 1988: 48).

Prigov himself, for instance, creates a distance to ideology by reproducing it in the perception of popular consciousness and not as it looks in the official code. His lyrical 'I' is often an average person situated in an over-ideologised reality who seeks as best he can to express the phenomena of life by means of various rather baroque clichés. But behind the absurdity there lies, nonetheless, a longing, as Ivor Severin says, for 'a lost harmony, an accord between fact and predicate' (Severin 1990: 225).

As official ideology was demolished, the postmodernists emerged to dance on the ruins. The first steps are indicated in a short story written in 1979 by Evgenii Popov where a gay man breaks his neck in an attempt to ascend a monumental sculpture of a he-man with an imposing chest (Popov 1990: 129-32). Viktor Erofeev similarly inspects the ruins and emerges with a grotesque trophy in his *A Life with an Idiot* (published in 1991), where a mystical red-headed stranger (a Soviet equivalent to Pasolini's *Teorema*) turns the life of an average Moscow couple upside down. The intruder, Volodia, resembles a cross between an ape and a 19th century bearded intellectual. Such works evidently periphrase and ridicule earlier norms.

So far, so good. We have overcome the straitjacket of the system, but what comes next? Seemingly, the former line of demarcation has been abolished. Indeed, by the end of the 1980s the exponents of the former underground culture had got access to Parnassus. A good sign of course, indicating the abolition of the formerly rigorous differentiation between the various layers of culture and an acceptance of the multiplicity of culture. As a nice example of border-crossing activity one might also mention an exhibition by the Moscow artist Andrei Monastyrskii and the British concept-artist Conrad Atkinson in the Avtozavodskaia subway station in July 1990. The underground had been recognized.

The New Context: Polyphony – Quantity or Quality?

If we look at the cultural scene on the threshold of the 1990s, we might be tempted to apply the term 'polyphony', used by the sculptor Ernst Neizvestny to define the essence of art. How fair is this? One thing is quantity, but what about quality, especially where 'polyphony' is regarded as a means to express the richness of the individual? One of the most famous works of art associated with renewal and perestroika is Abuladze's film *Repentance* (1987). With its surrealism and its sharp criticism of the Communist system it stands out as an expression of artistic freedom and civic courage. But the aim of the film was of course to show how hard it is to bury the dictator, to get rid of the totalitarian. The dictator rises repeatedly from his grave and continues to be an obstacle on the road to freedom. Perhaps the past is more implicit than we would like to think. It seems worth noting in this connection that the focus on the individual as such in the new art does not necessarily entail admiration for new individual personalities. On the contrary, many of the characters in these works of art are blocked and frustrated. Titles like *The Asthenic Syndrome* are quite characteristic as expressions of a mood that can be found, too, in the novels of the above-mentioned Kaledin and many others. A new term, *chernukha* has indeed been coined to describe works of art that deal with the ugly or profane. In this sense, it might seem wrong to postulate an essential change of consciousness or an inner renewal in society. The well-known film *Little Vera* surely deals more with the outer than with the inner, and here an even more pejorative term – *pornukha* – might be added to *cher-*

nukha. But the depiction of the seamy sides of life should not be taken only as a negative sign. The demolition of the self-sufficient monolith marks an end to one-sidedness, and it is not surprising if the individual, overwhelmed by information about the past and the outside world, may feel a bit lost. It is well known that a person who has spent a long time in prison can find it hard to get accustomed to freedom. Sometimes he may even long to get back to where he came from. But is not the registering of the cracks in the monolith preferable to attempts to mend the cracked surface? Acknowledging the warps and distortions in the apparently firm construction is the first condition for finding a way out. The artist who seeks to depict the lower depths (in a social and psychological sense) can in this respect be compared to the mole, constructing dark, subterranean corridors which do eventually lead to an exit. In this sense earthy, concrete criticism may contribute more to change than hollow slogans. In the 1930s, incidentally, Ernst Bloch objected as follows to Georg Lukacs' advocacy of socialist realism and his denunciation of expressionism:

> Is there not any dialectic connection between decline and rise? Is the bewildered, immature and incomprehensible necessarily <...> a sign of decadence? Could it not – in spite of simplified and hardly very revolutionary opinions – have a share in the transition from the old to the new world? At least in the struggle for this transition? Which only an immanent-concrete criticism instead of one founded on omniscient prejudices can further (Bloch 1976: 249).

The new art provides a starting point, and can be found on closer inspection to contain the germs of the formation of a new consciousness.

Which is not to say that it can't leave you rather depressed, as when, for instance, you encounter the school teacher Kolia (Nikolai) in Kira Muratova's film *The Asthenic Syndrome* (1989). The film represents a striking expression of resignation and defeatism. We are introduced to the main character in the metro, where he lies on the platform while people push past around him. It turns out that he is alive: he has merely fallen asleep. He gets up (otherwise there would be no movie), but it is extremely hard for him to keep his eyes open. After the initial surprise, one's attention is gradually hooked. Whether or not this was the director's intention, the film certainly suggests that Oblomov* has his descendants in the modern world. Kolia is a bad teacher, his pupils are bored and do not listen; we see him walking around in the streets, then resting on a bench, while someone shouts out that somebody's being killed; then he takes part – God knows why – in a seance in a bizarre circle with a young naked woman (where once again he falls asleep); he picks up the sound of a wind instrument – was it his mother showing off her musical skills? – playing, it seems, the song *I did it my way* (a grotesque allusion to the Brezhnev doctrine). We see, too, that he has a problem with his wife, but at least he is able to understand that she will be better off if he leaves her. Finally he meets, once more in the metro, a young girl who takes some interest in him. But this relationship fails to work out too, in so far as Kolia is unable to get up from his seat at the train's final stop; instead, he falls asleep, and thus ends up, literally as well as metaphorically, on a sidetrack. One way or another he seems doomed to stay in the underground. He appears to be stunned, seemingly unable ever to get up again. So here we find a kind of paralysis which is apparently also part of the general picture (and which can be interpreted as a sign of the social frustrations we have discussed).

We should therefore take a further look at phenomena which can be said to have risen to recognition in the new context. As far as the consolidation of alternative ideas or the emergence of a pluralistic context are concerned, the sceptic might point to a prominent new sign in Moscow life. In brief, the letter 'M'. Not the M that serves as an abbrevation for the subway, 'Metropoliten im. Lenina', but a new form of M, bright orange, and more oval in shape, the M which, as one Moscow author put it in 1990, shines 'high up in the air, above all our banners and flags' (L. L. 1990: 16). At the very place where The Lyre, the café immortalised by

---

* The passive protagonist in Goncharov's novel *Oblomov* (1859) – Ed.

the writer, V. Aksenov, once stood, a new establishment now sports its sign, described by the above-mentioned author as 'the tentacles of the capitalistic cuttle-fish': in other words, the sign of McDonald's. Thus, the symbol, so to speak, of the 'deeper-lying', underground plane – which as we have seen was much more complex than it might have seemed on the surface – has now not only been recognised, but has altered beyond recognition. But of course, we should not generalise from a single phenomenon. Looking around for other evidence in the cultural landscape, we soon come across another building, just as conspicuous, if not more so, in so far as it has risen on a formerly empty spot – or rather, on the site of a former swimming-pool. This is the cathedral of Christ the Saviour, once destroyed, now being re-erected. Here, too, there's cause for some surprise. The church undoubtedly has a symbolic value, but what exactly does it symbolise? Some would perhaps find it difficult even to establish the architectural value of the monument. Alexander Herzen, one might recall, dubbed the style of Nicholas I and Konstantin Ton (the architect) 'indo-byzantine' (Herzen 1969: 241). But at least one may say that this, too, is a sign of a trend whose relevance and actuality are open to question.

Conclusion

So what have we got? The choice between a "happy meal" and "salvation"? Of course, this is not the entire picture. But it is not hard to see a certain – unhappy – polarisation in Russian society today. This to a large degree can be traced to the conditions of debate, or rather the lack of such conditions, in the closed, totalitarian society. During perestroika certain underlying trends were activated, but because of a general uncertainty of direction these could not be discussed in a free, unprejudiced way. Moreover, the activation of these trends also revealed and intensified differences which had not previously been felt so markedly. As regards the substance of the alternative ideas which came to the surface (within the two-layer structure of the normative, or officially-accepted, culture on the one hand, and the suppressed, not openly articulated, but nevertheless differentiated spectrum of ideas on the other), this process could be illustrated with a definition from cognitive science:

> ...cognitive scientists working on expert knowledge have come to the realisation that knowledge is likely to consist of dissociated islands. Only when we become conscious of contradictions between the seperate cognitive islands do we realise the dissociation. If they are both unconscious, they can coexist quite happily (Baars 1994: 692).

With the possibility of articulation, these discords become clearer. But this manifestly calls for solution. It would not be wise to neglect certain issues, for in doing so we run the risk of one big levelling, be it so-called liberal or nationalistic.

During the 1995 election campaign, an American rap artist was invited to perform at a meeting of the party, Russia is our Home. Anything to attract new votes – but the performance proved a failure. The American rapper was confused, believing he'd been asked to participate in a concert, and the audience was similarly perplexed. So everyone was disappointed. As the *Herald Tribune* put it, commenting on the incident, 'Russia deserves something better'. (Needless to say, so did the rap artist and the audience in question.)

Questions of cultural heritage and freedom, i.e., of national identity and democracy, are interconnected, and only an unprejudiced discussion of all these issues, without exclusion, can bring forth solutions. The aim must surely be substantial renewal, multiplicity instead of levelling, individual creativity and social virtue, prosperity and stabilisation, as the condition for implementing the 'we-and-they principle', and including the new Russia in the world community.

Notes

1. See further my article 'Sider af sovjetkulturen i trediverne' (Aspects of Soviet Culture in the 1930s), *Slavica Othiniensia*, 14, 1994, pp. 9-27. A

thorough study of dualism in Soviet society can be found in Shlapentokh 1987.
2. The term *sobornost'* is not easy to translate. Elaborated in the period of Romanticism by the early Slavophiles (Khomiakov) as a word meaning 'unity in love', in the context of Orthodoxy, it has got a scale of connotations, ranging from the affirmation of 'the reality of freedom by widening the scope of freedom and by revealing its transcendent, universal dimension' (Berdiaev, *Dream and Reality*) to an ideological attribute in autocratic conceptions of conservatives (Ioann, *Triumphant Orthodoxy (Torzhestvo pravoslaviia)*, 1993). Here the term is used without its sometimes mythological loadedness, i.e., it becomes more or less equivalent to the rather neutral word 'communion'.
3. As a sign of the new atmosphere these extracts of Kabakov's *Memoirs* were published in the official magazine of the USSR Artists' Union, *Iskusstvo* 10, 1990. The issue was wholly devoted to underground art. In 1988, also in No. 10, the magazine presented trends among young artists, including comments on the cultural scene by older, 'established' underground artists.

References

Baars, B. J. and K. McGovern (1994) *Consciousness. AP Encyclopedia of Human Behavior,* vol. 1, p. 692.
Berdiaev, N. (1965) *Marx vs. Man*, in J. M. Edie, J. Scanlan and M-B. Zeldin, eds, *Russian Philosophy,* Vol. 3, Quadrangle, New York, pp. 156-66. (Originally published in 1938.)
Berdiaev, N. (1993) *O naznachenii cheloveka. Ekzistentsial'naia dialektika bozhestvennogo i chelovecheskogo,* Respublika, Moscow. (Paris 1931; 1947).
Berdiaev, N. (1990) 'Russkaia ideia', *Voprosy filosofii,* 1, 2, pp. 77-144; 87-154. (Originally 1946.)
Bloch, E. (1976) 'Diskussionen über Expressionismus', in O. F. Best, ed., *Theorie des Expressionismus,* Reclam, Stuttgart, pp. 241-54.
'D'iakon Vladimir Rusak' (1986) *Posev,* 6, pp. 32-33.
Erofeev, A. (1988) 'Metamorfozy "moskovskogo avangarda"', *Iskusstvo,* 10, pp. 42-47.
Erofeev, Ven. (1977) *Moskva-Petushki,* YMCA-Press. (First publication in the Soviet Union in the magazine *Trezvost' i kul'tura,* 12, 1988, 1-3, 1989.)
Erofeev, Vikt. (1991) *Zhizn' s idiotom,* SP Interbook, Moscow.
Frank, S. (1991) *Dukhovnye osnovy obshchestva,* 1st edn Paris 1930.

Frank, S. (1990) 'Po tu storonu pravogo i levogo', *Novyi mir,* 4, pp. 226-233. (Originally Paris 1931.)

Frank, S. (1965) 'Reality and Man. (Real'nost' i Chelovek)', in J. M. Edie, et al., eds, *Russian Philosophy,* vol. 3 , Quadrangle, New York, pp. 281-305.

Frank, S. (1990) *Sochineniia,* Moscow.

Herzen, A. (1969) *Byloe i dumy,* vol. 1, Moscow, pp. 238-249.

Kabakov, I. (1990) 'Iz vospominanii Il'i Kabakova', *Iskusstvo,* 10, pp. 6-10.

Kroeber, A. L. and C. Kluckhohn (1952) *Culture, A critical Review of Concepts and Definitions,* Cambridge, Mass.

L. L. (1990) 'Oskudeet li ruka daiushchego?', *Referendum. Zhurnal nezavisimykh mnenii,* 35, April, p. 15-16.

Neizvestny, E. (1989) 'O sinteze iskusstva', *Voprosy filosofii,* 7. (Written in the 1960s.)

Popov, E. (1990) 'Voskhozhdenie', *Vestnik novoi literatury,* pp. 129-32. (Written in 1979.)

Prigov, D. (1988) 'Dyshit, gde khochet i gde dyshitsia', *Iskusstvo,* 10, pp. 48-50.

Rubinstein, L. (1990) 'Predvaritel'noe predislovie k opytu kontseptual'noi slovesnosti', *Iskusstvo,* 10, pp. 47-8.

Severin, I. (1990) 'Novaia literatura 70-80-kh', *Vestnik novoi literatury,* pp. 222-39.

Shlapentokh, V. (1987) *Public Opinion and Ideology. Mythology and Pragmatism in Interaction,* Praeger, New York, London.

Trubetskoi, E. (1990) 'Vseobshchee, priamoe, tainoe i ravnoe' (1906), 'Staryi i novyi khristianskii messsianizm' (1912), 'O khristianskom otnoshenii k sovremennym sobytiiam' (1917), *Novyi mir,* 7, pp. 195-229.

Transition in Practice: Political Discourse and Market Patterns in Vilnius, Lithuania

PERNILLE LARSEN

> To start trading at Gariunai was a tragedy for me. I used to work in the theatre – I would never go and buy anything in Gariunai. People in artistic circles still consider that Gariunai represents something... I don't know, it immediately stamps a person – only people of a certain kind would trade there. But my friend, who used to work in the theatre with me, was bolder. She started first. She was on maternity leave, and afterwards she didn't come back to the theatre, but went on selling things at Gariunai. She suggested that I join her. The first day I had five sweaters in a bag and I kept one of them in my hand while walking around in Gariunai. I kept looking around anxiously, afraid of bumping into someone I knew. (Stase, market trader)

Gariunai market in Lithuania is one of the huge consumer markets that have grown out of 'the transition' in the former Soviet Union and Eastern Europe, providing the 'new poor' with various cheap consumer products. Here you can buy shoes and clothes, kitchen equipment, toys and much else, usually imported from Turkey, China, the United Arabic Emirates or Poland by market traders themselves. Gariunai is the largest wholesale market in the Baltic region.[1] An estimated 15,000 traders make a living from the market, and at present buyers come from Latvia, Belarussia and Ukraine as well as from other towns in Lithuania. The market was established in 1990, and until a few years ago, customers would come from as far away as Siberia and the Asian republics. Lately, visa restrictions between the former Soviet republics have put an end to much of this 'inter-republic' travel. However, the market still thrives, although profits are decreasing.[2]

But to trade at Gariunai is, as Stase's story indicates, a morally questionable activity and the market itself is regarded by Lithuanian society in general as being marginal, criminal and uncivilized. The market's transnational and 'ethnic' dimensions furthermore seem to establish it as a non-Lithuanian cultural space. Traders are often too ashamed to talk about their activities. When asked about their motives they state rather pragmatically: 'You've got to live somehow.' But why is market trade such a terrible form of activity, and why is the market regarded as less pure than other forms of business? Can this marginalization be viewed purely as a remnant of socialist ideas of trade, or is it a product of an emerging new moral economy? Finally, who are the people trading in this market and how do they cope with their dubious position, balancing on the edge of society?

In a wider perspective, the present chapter is an attempt to come to terms with 'the transition' from Communism to 'post-Communism' in the former Soviet Union. In doing so I shall draw upon previous anthropological and Soviet studies as well as on my own fieldwork among market traders in Vilnius in 1994 and 1995. The point I want to pursue is the contrast, or perhaps schism, between 'the transition' as represented through the various academic and political debates and 'transition' seen as everyday practice, especially that which is underprivileged and often silent within the political debates. I am particularly interested in strategies or 'tactics' which on the surface seem rather passive and dominated by other more powerful social and cultural fields, but which are actually more persistent and more innovative than they might seem at first glance (Michel de Certeau 1990). By analysing a particular market in Lithuania as such an underprivileged 'space', I believe it will be possible to examine critically some of our ideas and assumptions concerning what 'the Soviet transition' is all about.

The academic and political discourses on 'the transition' are dominated by a set of 'gate-keeping concepts' (Appadurai 1986). I shall begin by discussing the use of such concepts and the way they colour our understanding of contemporary post-Communist society by looking at three areas: the idea of Soviet society as rigidly separated into public and private social spaces; the idea of the transition as leading to a Western-type market; and finally discussions of 'nationalism' and 'national identity', especially important within Baltic studies, where nation-building and the establishment of new ethnic minorities have become key issues within both political and academic debate.

Remnants Of 'Soviet Studies' In 'Transition Studies'

Understanding 'Real Socialism': 'Public' Versus 'Private'
The distinct separation of society into two spheres of activity, one 'public' and one 'private', and furthermore the control exercised by 'public' over 'private' activities, have often been suggested as principal characteristics of Soviet society and Soviet-type systems.[3] As the Soviet system expected everybody to be committed to the well-being of the State, Soviet ideology gave priority to the individual's public role and duties over any form of private activity or interest. However, as an ironic result of the obvious widespread manipulation and control of cultural production and mistrust of the state, a large 'underground space' was created in which everybody was busy living their own lives, as well as establishing their own truths and norms (Bartusevicius 1993). Although views have varied as to the extent of public control over individual and private lives, duality as a structuring principle in Soviet-type societies has prevailed. Especially within the anthropology of socialism this has been central (e.g. Shlapentokh 1988, Kenedi 1982, Bartusevicius 1993, Sampson 1987, Mars and Altman 1983). Furthermore, it seems that most anthropologists have been more preoccupied with private 'underground' practices than with public discourse (see for example Wedel 1986 and 1992 or Kenedi 1982). These studies have recently been criticized – and I think rightly – for presenting the ideology of socialism as an empty shell, in comparison with widespread private and anti-socialist activities, as well as for failing to investigate how and when people managed to shift between the various spaces. (Sampson 1991). More importantly, however, these studies highlight the problematic assumption that private activities are more 'real' and closer to the 'truth' of socialism than the 'faked' public discourse. Such a viewpoint maintains that

the public face of socialism was, for most people, a mere act of ritualism, and that socialist discourse as such never penetrated into people's private lives and habitus. In this case, the analytical distinction thus reflects an ideological position. Life in Soviet-style societies seems rather to have been characterized (as in most other societies) by the ability to deal with an ambivalence between communal and individual morality. Instead of taking the problematic epistemological position of viewing the public/private dichotomy *a priori* as an explanatory framework, I shall suggest, along with Chris Hann (1994), Steven Sampson (1991), that we need to scrutinize very carefully the various and shifting contexts of private and public social spaces. The techniques of dealing with moral ambivalence in particular need to be examined in order to understand the 'politics' of 'public' and 'private' activities.

When moving on to 'transition studies', there seems to be an assumption here that a successful transition will entail a specific form of change in the relationship between 'public' and 'private' social spaces and the establishment of a more Western-style balance between public discourse and private practice. As Verdery expresses it:

> ...because Marxism-Leninism will no longer be enforcing transformations of consciousness, consciousness will come to be formed less through discourse and more through practices... (Verdery 1991: 434)

But such a substitution of public discourse by private practice need not necessarily be an outcome of 'the transition'. On the contrary, the ambivalence of public and private conduct continues to be important, although the borders between their contexts are becoming blurred and new fields of ambivalence are being created in relation to the establishment of new 'public', 'semi-public' and 'private' spaces.

The Myth Of The Western Market
'Is the bazaar a market?' The question is raised in a discussion concerning the (mis)understanding of, and the political/ethical

problems involved in, Western economic 'assistance' to Eastern Europe and Russia (Gerner & Hedlund 1994). Not surprisingly, the answer to the question is negative, and Gerner and Hedlund use the development of a wild bazaar economy in Russia as an example of how Western economic experts and politicians have failed to give their Eastern European counterparts adequate assistance. Gerner and Hedlund are therefore on the whole highly critical of what they conceive as the unrealistic project of transforming the former Soviet Union into an ideal model of late American capitalist society, their main argument being that modern versions of the neo-classical economic paradigm completely ignore the historical foundations of the economy in the West. They maintain that the whole project of rapid systemic transformation in Eastern Europe was totally unrealistic from the outset. There is no single ready-made version of Western society, and even if there were, it would be unrealistic to assume that it could be easily transferrable to a radically different socio-cultural context.

However, it is not only within the Western economic discourse of the market that the cultural and historical context is ideologically coloured. If we turn to local political discussions in various post-Communist countries in Europe the attitudes are the same, though for different reasons. As soon as Communism as an ideological superstructure and administrative/legal system is suspended, the 'return to Europe' is considered to be an automatic and much desired outcome. In both cases 'the transition' is assumed to lead to a development away from post-Communist states towards modern, Western-style societies. In addition, there is a general assumption (which is empirically unaccounted for) that 'the market' will automatically lead to increased prosperity in Eastern Europe.[4] Thus the development of a Western-style market is also assumed to include a Western living standard.

When looking at the empirical example of market trade in Lithuania, such developments seem far from realistic. But instead of regarding bazaar economy as a form of failed market or intermediate step on the assumed road towards a 'real' market (as Gerner and Hedlund implicitly do in their critique of the bazaar), I suggest such practices simply exemplify a different kind of economic development and that they do indeed illuminate 'the local practice model' (Gudeman 1992).

New Baltic Battlefields
The Baltic countries are heavily influenced by the rhetoric of 'returning to Europe', which plays an important part in the national rhetoric of transition all over Eastern Europe. An obsession with European civilization and a claim to be developing towards the West have been noted by Holy in respect of Czechoslovakia (1992), suggested by Sievert Nielsen (1995) as applicable to Russia and believed by Buchowski (1993) to be specific for Poland.

The West for its part has shown considerable interest in the Baltic states. This interest is reflected in political initiatives as well as in cultural studies. The Baltic states have been regarded as the 'motor' in dismantling the former Soviet Union, and as all three countries do have quite large minority populations, nationalism and ethnic minorities have quickly become key issues. Even when taking into account the importance that revived national symbols play in the political life of the Baltic states, there is a striking degree of preoccupation with public rituals and political rhetoric within the field of Baltic studies. Nation-building is discussed in relation to the present use of past symbols and there is little discussion of individual interpretations of such symbols. Åke Norborg, for example, has written about the continuous but shifting importance of song festivals in establishing political legitimacy in Lithuania before, during and after Soviet rule, and Pål Kolstø demonstrates how national symbols from the interwar period have undergone a tremendous revival and emotional coding in all three Baltic states (Norborg 1993, Kolstø 1995). Although these analyses are highly interesting and give insight into formal political/ritual changes from Sovietism to nationalism, the preoccupation with the national political level seems to divert attention from other, less articulated social spaces, especially those considered to be unimportant, or perhaps antagonistic to national-political goals.

To a large extent the same formalism seems to characterize the field of national minorities, where researchers' interest by and large has followed political and 'primordial' definitions of ethnicity (see for example Andersen 1995, Krag 1992, Nørgaard (ed.) 1994, Raun 1994). Such analyses run the risk of reproducing politically and ideologically 'frozen' ethnic categories, and in the case of the Baltic states, could serve to reinforce potential ethnic conflicts. In addition to such studies of national ethnic politics we need to examine what is going on beneath the national political level and investigate how various parts of a given population deal with ethnic relations in their daily lives, as well as how and when such categories change.

Finally, the main obstacles to nation-building today need not lie in the existence of large minority groups (as is often claimed in national political discourse) but in trying to establish a culturally homogeneous national state in an age of globalization:

> Estonia is restoring herself as a nation-state. Although it is quite possible that the mission of nation-states has been exhausted, at least in Western Europe (as some theorists argue), Estonia cannot jump from the sub-national (sub-state) level to a transnational one. It is obvious that Estonians cannot by-pass the national level without endangering their ethnic identity (Ruutsoo 1993: 95).

This passage from Ruutsoo indicates the tension between the political goals of the Baltic states and their actual situation. Although there are obvious political reasons for underestimating the 'globalized' aspects of newly independent states, we need not do so analytically. Within Western Europe, studies of national identity and ethnic minorities increasingly focus on transnational integration, symbolic ethnicity, the manipulation of ethnic symbols and trans-ethnicity (see for example Gans 1979, Roosen 1989, Larsen 1994). Such concepts may shed new light on emerging social identities in Eastern Europe as well.

I have so far indicated some of the problems involved in the use of 'Soviet and post-Soviet' gate-keeping concepts. My main point of criticism is that they transfer existing political categories to an analytical level. In this way they may obscure our understanding of the socio-cultural and political processes that are taking place in the 'real transition'. An examination of the transition in practice, however, sheds new light on our discussion.

Gariunai: A Symbolically 'Marked' Market

Although the Gariunai market is huge and provides tens of thousands of people with a daily income, the market has, along with other non-food markets in Lithuania, a very bad reputation. Criticism is levelled at various aspects: the market is uncivilized and dominated by racketeers and thieves; traders just stand there, they don't do real work; incomes are not declared, thus trade is black; the market is considered non-Lithuanian, and to be dominated by Poles and Russians; it is outdoor and often dirty (one's shoes get dirty), and finally the goods are of poor quality and traders often cheat. Furthermore, a continuous impoverishment of the market has recently taken place; profits are diminishing, while at the same time new groups of the population are entering the market, often forced by increasing (though largely hidden) unemployment in Lithuania. Many teachers, technicians and even a few artists (many of them women) have lately begun trading. This development has further influenced the status of the market. But although all these criticisms of the market contain elements of truth, the process of marginalization, symbolically as well as economically, seems to be more complex and in addition highly political; there is indeed more to it than dirty shoes.

The 'Private' Going 'Public'

Rasa's story:
> I started my business long ago, about 1984. I was knitting at home and then selling. The government called it speculation. People didn't call it that. Later I started to sew. There were a lot of fashionable things from Poland at that time, so I would put 'made in Poland' labels on the clothes. Later on the government would allow us to trade, and I got a licence for producing and selling. I started to sell my things in the Kalvariu market. The first time it was terrible. I remember finding a very small chair to sit on, so that it would be difficult to see me behind the table. I found it so embarrassing. At that time a woman in the market was called *turgaus boba* (Lithuanian for 'market bitch'). It wasn't very respectable, but we needed the money. ...I would go to the market every morning at 7 o'clock

except on Mondays. I would get sewing materials from Moscow and then sell from the tables at Kalvariu.

Later, when I found out that there were also doctors and teachers in the market, it became easier for me.

In 1989-1990 I was trading in Kalvariu and in Eisiskes... mostly in dresses and skirts for women.

Later, when the market moved to Gariunai in 1990, I sewed at home and traded at Gariunai. We didn't have a car, so my mother would drive me to the market with my big bags.

After some time I wanted to try to find an easier way of making money. It was too hard, I was trading during the day... sleeping a little bit after I returned and then in the evening and at night I would sew for the next day. I thought that going to Turkey and bringing goods back would be an easier way. I was very nervous the first time, but I made friends on the plane. Later I started selling leather jackets. All leather jackets at Gariunai come from Turkey, even those with 'made in Germany' or 'made in Italy' labels (Rasa, former market trader).

As the market only came into being in 1990, it can be viewed as a very visible sign of political and economic change as well as a result of the opening of the former firmly closed Soviet borders. When Gariunai was first established, Lithuania was still a part of the Soviet Union. The market developed as a consequence of the opening of the Polish borders in 1989 and the possibility of getting goods from Poland into Lithuania. Thus the people in the market were mainly Polish traders and Russian customers, although some locals also participated. Polish traders imported goods from Turkey or Thailand and sold them at Gariunai, where they were available to the Soviet Union as a whole.

It would be misleading, however, to depict Gariunai entirely as a novelty, since many traders have experience of past (illegal) forms of underground production and trading, and the association between trade and 'speculation' is still significant. Thus when asked about the history of the market, traders usually explained that the market began as *talkucke*, an 'illegal place for speculation'. Gradually it established itself as a part of Kalvariu, the main food market in Vilnius. After some time the trade was moved outside the centre of the city, at first to a location near the airport and then finally to Gariunai, which is situated on the main road to Kaunas, about 10 km from the centre of Vilnius. This development reveals not only how the market was first established as a place, but also during the process was removed from the centre of the city and re-established far outside it.

Apart from illustrating physically the marginal position that the Gariunai market occupies in Lithuanian society, the very establishment of Gariunai as a place seem to have further stigmatized market activity. Rasa, quoted above, is not only ashamed, but refuses to be seen, as she hides behind her goods in the market. The forced publicity of traders in the market (for one has to be visible in order to sell anything at all), demands new tactics, and most traders struggle to remain socially invisible as such. Quite a large number have a formal public job from which they earn practically nothing, but which provides them with a front to cover their role as market trader. Others, for example traders from provincial towns, drive hundreds of kilometres each day to Gariunai in order not to be seen trading in their home town. By establishing Gariunai as a place, speculation, traditionally carried out secretly, all of a sudden not only became legalized in a (partially) publically owned market, but also visible by occupying a public social space. This involves revealing activities which, although widespread in Soviet society as well, by and large remained hidden until the market was established as a physical place.[5]

But although 'unwanted publicity' is an important point in understanding the marginalization of Gariunai, the market is not easily defined as an entirely public space. In fact it seems difficult to place Gariunai within either a 'public' or a 'private' social field. The social space that it represents might more adequately be characterized as layers of public, semi-public, semi-private and private spaces. There is an official administrator, who is supposed to sell the trading places and keep some order in the whole area. In reality he has little power. For example, he doesn't control the selling of trading-places in the market. In order to buy a trading-place, a would-be trader needs to have personal connections and thereby to find someone – usually in one of the various racketeer groups – who exercises the real control over a given part of the market. Thus private networks are a *sine qua non* for being in the market, and in order to get information about prices, goods and available trading-places, traders are dependent on close personal contacts. By far the commonest way to start trading would be to go with somebody else the first time and be advised as to what to buy and from whom. Viewed from ground level, the market is thus a mixture of public and private structures. In this light Gariunai therefore appears as a shifting or altering space; borders between the various social spaces are relatively blurred.

The Uncivilized Market
Gariunai market clashes in several ways with the idea of transition as a more or less autonomous development of a Western-style market. As mentioned above, there are racketeers or semi-legal power structures in the market. As one trader put it:

> At Gariunai there are different groups of racketeers, and they ask a lot of money. I know 'the Boas', 'the Sportsmen' 'the Blacks', 'the Grey-haired', 'the Greens' and 'the Elephants' (I myself pay 'the Blacks')...' (Vytenis, market trader).

As everybody knows about the racketeers, their authority is seldom questioned. Actually the racketeers have gradually consolidated their authority to the extent that in order to occupy a place, traders need to buy a sort of licence from them. Traders then pay their 'tributes' three months in advance. The racketeers have established themselves as the real rulers of the market, and have further institutionalized their power by buying up parts of the market such as several areas for private parking, and monopolizing certain (illegal) forms of trade. Their activities and influence can be viewed as an example of 'the transition' being more violent, and less automatic, than hitherto assumed.

But the market is not the only place, characterized by power struggles and alternative forms of privatization. In general, the Lithuanian economy can be regarded as a highly contested field. The very marginalization of Gariunai can be regarded as a sign of this contestation, for other more influential 'mafias' struggle to monopolize important economic niches within the national economy.[6] As Algis, a rather successful market trader, explains:

> We can't do business outside Gariunai. If I wanted to buy a shop in Vilnius... It's easy to find premises – no problem. But it's difficult to open a shop because, for example, if I wanted to open a shop in Vokieciu Street and wanted to start trading in jeans, traders, or people from, for example, Londvil, who are also trading in jeans, simply wouldn't let me do so. It's because of corruption... big corruption. They have friends in the economic police or in the Fire Brigade... They would find a reason to close my shop. I would have big problems – they would come and check my business. Of course I would like to open a shop, because the prices in town are much better, but I can't handle this kind of business. (Algis, market trader)

As Lithuanian legislation is complicated and often contradictory, it is always possible to detect some violation of the law. Newcomers without connections will be unable to bribe or negotiate their way out again. Seen in this light economic practices in Gariunai do not seem fundamentally different from or more criminal than that of more 'established' businesses outside the market. The Gariunai market would appear to be, not blacker, but rather a different shade of black compared with more prestigious businesses down town.

The social marginalization of the market seems to cover an economic struggle currently taking place and forming part of the 'real economic transition'.

Finally, as Rasa's story indicates, apart from the Western labels in Turkish and Asian clothes, and the widespread practice of using US dollars as currency, there is nothing Western about the market – something which might further devalue its status, since it contradicts the idea of a 'return to Europe' as a common national goal. Traders are oriented towards Asia and to some extent Poland, and their ideas of trade as well as their networks are influenced by this Asian orientation.

The Contrast Between National Identity And Local Reality

Within the national discourse, e.g. that prevalent in national political debates or in national newspapers, the Gariunai market is often not considered as part of the national Lithuanian project of 'transition'. The fact that most traders, although regarding themselves as Lithuanians and possesing Lithuanian citizenship, are highly critical of the Lithuanian state and administration and moreover constantly move in and out of the country, does not seem to make the relationship any the less strained. A main point of discussion within the political rhetoric seems to be the non-Lithuanian dimension of the market.

At present, although Poles (and Russians) are now almost absent from the market, traders stressed their business strategies as 'Polish-style trading' and recognized the influence that Poles had had on this form of trade.

> It is pure Polish style to take advantage of the differences in price level in various countries. The Poles would make prices equal in all the countries they went to. First the Poles went to Lithuania, then Lithuanians went to Poland, and then Belarussians went to Lithuania (Algis E. market trader).

Interestingly, local traders generally maintain that Polish trade has now become more civilized, often assuming that Lithuanian trading practices will follow the same line of development. Polish traders are generally regarded as more specialized and richer, and Poles are furthermore said to have developed trading networks further to the East, for example with Taiwan, Korea and Indonesia. But apart from this, the close Polish contact has heavily involved local Lithuanian Poles in the market trade. Thus about a third of market traders are local Poles, a third local Russians and a third Lithunanians.[7] Many traders moreover suggested to me that Lithuanians in general have started later, especially in comparison with the Poles. But although the political rhetoric concerning Gariunai focuses on the non-Lithuanian aspect of the market, this is seldom seen as being in any way problematic by traders, Lithuanians, or non-Lithuanians alike. On the contrary, most informants would deliberately downplay the ethnic differences in the market and term everybody 'locals'. Thus the statement 'he is a Pole' indicates that a given person is from Poland, and would never be said about a 'Lithuanian Pole'. Many Lithuanians who have been trading with Poland seem to have learned to speak

Polish quite well. Discussions with traders furthermore revealed several cases where ethnic distinctions made no sense. Quite a few traders were unwilling to categorize themselves within any one ethnic group at all, but claimed simply to be 'locals'. Many of these were the children of mixed Polish/Russian marriages. When asked about their native language, they often said Russian, although one or even both parents were Poles. In general many local Poles, having attended Russian schools, often speak both Polish and Lithuanian poorly.

This makes no difference to their ability to trade, since the market language is mainly Russian. Russian appears to be a necessary means of communication with customers from former Soviet Republics, including the other Baltic states. Furthermore, the use of Russian helps to 'depoliticize' ethnic relations within the market, as it is known by everybody involved.

Apart from the obvious necessity of knowing Russian, the ability to deal with pluralism and communicate inter-ethnically is an important resource in the market. Traders deal with Russian, Baltic and other non-Lithuanian customers, and are also obliged to deal with Turkish, Chinese or Polish suppliers. In fact the ability to 'communicate' was considered to be the central human resource in the market. Significantly, although language competence represents an important economic factor, it is not recognized as such by traders. In this way, part of the trans-ethnic competence remains unarticulated.

Conceptualizing 'The Transition'

I have suggested that we need to transcend some of the 'gatekeeping concepts' prevalent in the political and academic field of transition in order to understand contemporary post-Soviet society. By using the Gariunai market as an example, and examining market practices as well as the national discourse on market trade, I have discussed some of the social and cultural processes that are at present taking place in Lithuania.

The Gariunai market and its traders are regarded by the general public as being marginal – and the marginalization is constantly being reproduced: economically, socially and morally. By focusing on trading practices, however, it becomes clear that many of these practices are not confined to the market, but are widespread in the rest of Lithuanian society as well. Thus the market, in terms of a specific set of practices and a certain economic style, appears more marginal than it really is. In fact I suggest that one reason for the continous marginalization of the market is precisely because it reveals practices that are also prevalent, though hidden, elsewhere. In this sense one could argue that Gariunai is private practice that has surfaced and become public, a form of behaviour that is stigmatized because of being conducted in the wrong (public) place. Actually, the visibility of trade and trading practices is often put forward by critics as an argument against it. Statements such as: 'it looks dirty', 'they stand in the open air', etc., all have something to do with revealing what should remain hidden. It is difficult, however, to regard the market as being altogether public. Although officially recognized as a trading-place, much of what takes place in Gariunai is completely concealed from visitors, and semi-legal power structures in the market make it inaccessible to outsiders. All in all, though distinctions between public and private conduct remains the establishment of new public, private and semi-public spaces has blurred the dichotomy.

Thus the market cannot be interpreted entirely as 'underground economy' becoming public and visible. It can only be understood by looking at the role it plays in the restructuring of contemporary society. The marginalization of the market highlights the establishment of new social and economic spaces and the power struggle that this implies. Furthermore, the market can be viewed both as a sign of the opening of borders, and of the impoverishment which seems to be inherent in 'the transition' as well. I suggest that the market can be seen as what Hylland Eriksen has termed a 'cultural crossroad... where (cultural) streams meet, mingle, contrast, influence each other and produce new reactions' (Hylland Eriksen 1994: 6, my translation). Customers come from all over the Baltic region, traders go abroad to Poland and Asia to buy their wares, and since they often sell them through privately-owned shops or indoor markets in Vilnius, the Gariunai market is certainly not the 'island' it might seem to be. But the kind of globalization it represents is of a different nature from what is usually indicated by the term (e.g. Hannerz 1987; 1990) as the West is almost entirely absent from the scene (although, from time to time it may be hiding backstage). Places like Gariunai might be difficult to come to terms with for Lithuanians and Westerners alike, because they are visible signs of a very different kind of 'transition' from what was expected and accepted. But they are significant, precisely because they contradict the ideology of 'the transition' in several ways. They challenge academic and political discourse on the transition by questioning the political project of a homogenous nation state, the creation of a Western-style market and the possibility of achieving a Western living standard. On the contrary, the use of the Russian language, the prevalence of multi-ethnicity and traders' trans-ethnic and Asian orientation give it a distinct flavour of a sort of globalized Sovietism, and indeed there seems to be very little 'Western' about it at all.

The national political discourse involves the creation of a national community understood as a bound and reasonably homogenous cultural space. In Lithuania, as well as in the other Baltic states, the political project has been almost entirely founded on history. Present nationalist identity is based on a historical tradition, solely stemming from the interwar period and earlier Lithuanian history. The national political project has been to establish a feeling of cultural continuity by disregarding the last 50 years of Sovietism. In the political rhetoric of transition, concepts such as 'remnants of socialism' and 'post-Sovietism' have a definitely negative ring to them. Instead, the national idea has been projected as a copy of an ideal type of Western society based on selected periods of Lithuanian history. This is, I suggest, what Gariunai contradicts.

A study of the market practice questions the political as well as academic assumptions of nation states as bound entities, and the assumed process of Westernization. Frequent statements by traders, such as 'we are all locals', furthermore suggested that ethnic relations in practice, also look different from those represented in the dominant ideology. Cultural resources for trans-ethnic communication are important in the multi-ethnic market. This ability to deal with, and at times disregard, ethnic differences seems at least partly to originate from the Soviet period. The Russian language is one resource in this respect, although the ability to communicate in Russian is apparently taken so much for granted that none of the traders regarded this as a resource at all. Finally, a form of globalization can be said to take place, as traders move around in the world and establish new networks. They inevitably take part in the creation of what is generally termed trans-national or global spaces (Appadurai 1990).

This is not in the least surprising, since sociologists and anthropologists alike have turned to concepts like 'globalization', 'diaspora', 'creolization' and 'deterritorialization' in order to come to terms with modern or postmodern reality (Featherstone and Appadurai 1990, Hannerz 1992). It would therefore seem more peculiar if the 'opening' of Eastern parts of Europe and the former Soviet Union were not to result in processes of this very kind. Empirically, there seems to be little difference, and I maintain that 'the transition' in the form of the actual opening of borders, new global relationships and general internationalization does imply globalization, although Western influence is less than presumed. The actual orientation towards the former Soviet Union and Asia also seems to be connected with the fact that 'the opening of borders' has so far taken place in this direction, yet (as traders express it) 'the wall has been rebuilt towards the West'. The development in Gariunai, which in many ways reflects that of Lithuanian society in general, does not point purely towards Westernization.[8] By focusing on practice when developing an adequate analytical framework for conceptualizing 'the transition' in Eastern Europe and former Soviet Union – however this transition may turn out – we are unavoidably made aware of such signs of globalization and modernization.

Notes

1. The present article is based on data from a recent 8-month period of fieldwork in Vilnius, Lithuania in 1994-95. The overall aim of this research was to shed light on the strategies and ideology of the participants in, and 'constructors' of, the free market, the entrepreneurs. My data from the market consist of participant observation, ethnographic interviewing

with market traders, a survey of 135 traders and interviews with a number of other Vilnius traders and entrepreneurs. Lithuanian newspaper articles about Gariunai in *Lietuvos Rytas* and *Respublika* in the period 1989-95 have also been drawn upon.
2. Traders at Gariunai talk about how a wall has been 'built' and not how the wall 'came down', which is our image in the West. Most of them regard their actual possibilities of travelling to the West as well as to the CIS countries as being highly restricted.
3. According to Shlapentokh, 'public' activities can be defined as 'those activities and institutions that pursue social and national goals...' (Shlapentokh, 1988: 1). The term 'public' is mostly related to the central government and its agencies. This means it is often used in much the same sense as 'official'. The terms 'private' and 'public' are antonyms. The designation 'private' covers 'any activity of single individuals or organizations in pursuing goals' (ibid: 4).
4. At the conference, "Soviet Civilization", in Odense, where this paper was originally presented, the economist Hans Aage referred to an article in the Danish newspaper *Politiken*, where Poland was proclaimed a 'Wirtschaftswunder' at a time when all economic reports on the Polish economy pointed to serious problems.
5. In late Soviet society everyone just knew where to find the black marketeers – they needed no publicity (see for example Fisher 1993).
6. Most shops in Vilnius also pay 'protection money' to racketeers, although I have no way of knowing whether these are the same groups as those operating at Gariunai. The term 'mafia' was often used in this way by traders themselves when describing the Lithuanian economic environment.
7. As no official data are available, I refer to my own questionnaire covering 135 traders at Gariunai.
8. There are of course very clear signs of influence from the West, but if one disregards the large Western chains and focuses on local entrepreneurs, many of them are neither influenced by, nor trading with, the West, but are oriented towards Russia or the Far East.

References

Alexander, P. (1992) 'What's in a price?', in R. Dilley, ed., *Contesting Markets: Analyses of Ideology, Discourse and Practice,* Edinburgh University Press, Edinburgh.

Andersen, E. A. (1995) 'Arbejdsløshed blandt russere i Estland', *Nordisk Østforum*, no. 2.
Appadurai, A., ed. (1986) *The Social Life of Things*, Cambridge University Press, Cambridge, pp. 3-64.
Appadurai, A. (1990) 'Disjuncture and Difference in the Global Cultural Economy', in M. Featherstone, ed., *Global Culture. Nationalism, Globalization and Modernity*, Sage Publications, London, Newbury Park and New Delhi.
Bartusevicius, V. (1993) 'Socializmo Liekanos Lietuvos Zmoniu Santykiuose', *I Laisve*, vol. 117, Nov.
Buchowski, M. (1994) 'From anti-communist to post-communist ethos: the case of Poland', *Social Anthroplogy*, vol. 2, no. 2, pp. 133-148.
de Certeau, M. (1988) *The Practice of Everyday Life*, Berkeley University Press, Berkeley.
Featherstone, ed., (1990) *Global Culture. Nationalism, Globalization and Modernity*, Sage Publications, London, Newbury Park and New Delhi, pp. 1-14.
Fisher, L. (1993) *Survival in Russia. Chaos and Hope in Everyday Life*, Westview Press, Boulder.
Gans, H. J. (1979) 'Symbolic Ethnicity. The Future of Ethnic Groups and Cultures in America', *Ethnic and Racial Studies*, vol. 12, no. 1, London.
Gerner, K. & S. Hedlund (1994) 'Homo Oeconomicus Meets Homo Sovieticus', *Sisällys*, no. 1.
Gudeman, S. (1992) 'Markets, Models and Morality', in R. Dilley, ed., *Contesting Markets. Analyses of Ideology, Discourse and Practice*, Edinburgh University Press, Edinburgh.
Hann, C. M. (1992) 'Market Principle, Market-place and the Transition in Eastern Europe', in R. Dilley, ed., *Contesting Markets. Analyses of ideology, Discourse and Practice*, Edinburgh University Press, Edinburgh.
Hann, C. M. (1994) 'After Communism: reflections on East European anthropology and 'the transition'', *Social Anthropology*, vol. 2, no. 3, pp. 229-49.
Holy, S. (1992) 'Culture, Market Ideology and Economic Reform in Czechoslovakia', in R. Dilley, ed., *Contesting Markets. Analyses of Ideology, Discourse and Practice*, Edinburgh University Press, Edinburgh.
Hylland-Eriksen, T. (1995) *Kulturelle Veikryss. Essays om kreolisering*, Universitetsforlaget, Oslo, pp. 5-43.
Kenedi, J. (1982) *Do it Yourself. Hungary's Hidden Economy*, Pluto Press.
Kolstø, P. (1995) 'Nasjonsbyggning i Eurasia', *Nordisk Østforum*, no. 1.
Krag, H. (1992) 'Det baltiske dilemma, minoritetskonflikt i Estland', in E. A. Andersen, ed., *Minoriteternes situation og rettigheder i de baltiske lande*, ICØ, Copenhagen.

Larsen, P. (1995) 'Hebben Nederlanders dan geen cultuur? Een beschouwing over Nederlands onderzoek naar 'etnisch ondernemerschap", *Tien Jaar Migrantenstudies,* no. 1.

Mars, G. & Y. Altman (1983) 'The Cultural Basis of Soviet Georgia's Second Economy', *Soviet Studies,* vol. 35, no. 4.

Norborg, Å. (1993) *Song Festivals and Politics. The Manipulation of National Symbols in Lithuania,* unpublished manuscript.

Nørgaard, O., ed. (1994) *De baltiske lande efter uafhængigheden. Hvorfor så forskellige?* Politica, Århus.

Raun, T. U. (1994) 'Ethnic Relations and Conflict in the Baltic States', in W. R. Duncan & G. P. Holman, Jr., eds, *Ethnic relations and Regional Conflict. The Former Soviet Union and Yugoslavia,* Westview Press, Boulder.

Roosens, E. (1989) *Creating Ethnicity. The Process of Ethnogenesis,* Sage Publications, London.

Ruutsoo, R. (1993) 'The Transformation of Estonia into a Nation-State and the Search for a new Identity', in I. Alanen, ed., *The Baltic States at a Crossroads: Preliminary Methodological Analysis,* University of Jyväskylä, Jyväskylä.

Sampson, S. (1987) 'The Second Economy of the Soviet Union and Eastern Europe', *The Annals of the American Academy of Political and Social Science,* vol. 493.

Sampson, S. (1991) 'Is There an Anthropology of Socialism?', *Anthropology Today,* vol. 7, no. 5.

Shlapentokh, V. (1989) *Public and Private Life of the Soviet People. Changing Values in Post-Stalin Russia,* Oxford University Press, New York and Oxford.

Sievert Nielsen, F. (1994) 'Rapport fra Forskerkurset. Continuity and Change in Post-Soviet societies', *Antropolognytt,* no. 2.

Verdery, K. (1991) 'Theorizing socialism: a prologue to the 'transition', *American Ethnologist,* vol. 18, no. 3, pp. 419-440.

Wedel, J. (1986) *The Private Poland,* Facts on File Publications, New York and Oxford.

Wedel, J., ed. (1992) *The Unplanned Society. Poland During and after Communism,* Columbia University Press, New York, pp. 1-21.

Notes on Contributors

Hans Henrik Brockdorff gained his Ph.D. from Odense University, Denmark. He has translated several novels from Russian into Danish and has published articles on aspects of Soviet culture. He is currently preparing his thesis on Russian culture and consciousness for publication.

Mette Bryld is Associate Professor at the Department of Slavonic Studies, Odense University, Denmark. She teaches Russian culture and is currently doing research on the re-invention of wilderness in the late twentieth century.

Søren Damkjaer has a MA degree in Sociology from the University of Copenhagen, Denmark, where he is now Associate Professor in Movement Studies and the Sociology of Sport. Research areas include sociology of the body, cultural studies and sociology of sport.

David Gillespie has a Ph.D. from Leeds University, England. He has taught Russian language and literature at Bath University since 1985, and has published a number of books and articles on Russian literature and cinema.

Natal'ia Kozlova is a leading researcher at the Institute of Philosophy at the Russian Academy of Science (RAN) and Professor at the Department of Philosophy at the Russian State University of Humanities (RGGU). She has published on mass consciousness, on the culture of everyday life and other socio-cultural matters.

Erik Kulavig has a Ph.D. in Russian studies and is Associate Professor at the Department of Slavonic Studies, Odense University, Denmark. He has published on Soviet-Russian culture and is currently working on the history of Russian society in the Khrushchev period.

Pernille Larsen graduated as an anthropologist from the University of Copenhagen, Denmark, in 1992. She is now a research fellow at the Institute of Anthropology where she is writing her dissertation on market, traders and trading strategies in contemporary Lithuania.

Irina Sandomirskaya is a Candidate of Philological Sciences and a Fellow at the Institute of Linguistics of the Russian Academy of Sciences. The area of her research is the interaction between language and culture, and the cultural connotation as a constituent of a linguistic sign. She is currently engaged in two projects on language, culture and identity.

Ol'ga Velikanova graduated from the Deparenent of History, Leningrad University. For ten years she worked at the State Museum of Political History in St. Petersburg. Her Ph.D. dissertation (1993) was devoted to the cult of Lenin in Soviet Russia. She is a researcher at the Independent Academy of Humanities in St. Petersburg and continues to study the problems of Soviet public consciousness.

Natal'ia Zhuravkina was educated at the Lenin Pedagogical University in Moscow. She has taught Russian language at the Moscow Pushkin Russian Language Institute, and since 1991 has been affiliated to Bath University, England. She has published articles on Russian cinema, and is currently writing a doctorate on the plays of A. Ostrovskii.

Index

A

Abdrashitov, Vadim, 140, 141
Abuladze, Tengiz, 140, 141, 157
Academy of Medical Sciences, 58
Academy of Sciences, 56, 58
Adzhubei, 85
Afinogenov, A., 58
Aksenov,V., 160
All-Russian Ministry of Physical Culture, 116
Anarchism or Socialism, 57
Andrei Rublev, 138
Anikushin, 32
Armand, Inessa, 36
Arshavskii, I.A, 54
Ascent, The, 144
Asthenic Syndrome, The, 157, 158
Asya's Happiness, 137
Atkinson, Conrad, 157

B

Bel'kovich, V., 69
Benjamin, Walter, 40
Berdiaev, N., 150; on Communism, 149
Bloch, Ernst, 158
Body, the: as index of cultural change, 131, 132; control of, 118, 119-20, 122, 132; culture of, 117, 118; dimensions of, 117, 121, 122, 123; discipline of, 120; discourse of, 45, 49; in the modernisation process, 117; individual, 118, 119, 129-30; institutions of, 117, 118, 120, 121, 122, 123, 125, 126, 131; new Russian, 116; post-Soviet, 116; programmes for management of, 119; regulation of, 118, 122, 124; sociology of, 117, 120-21, 131, 132; Soviet, 116, 131; transformation of, 120; under socialism, 115
Bodily behaviour, 124
Bolsheviks, the, 78, 119, 149
Braginskii, Emil', 143
Brezhnev, Leonid, 109, 111; doctrine, 159
Bulgakov, Sergei, 150
Burnt By The Sun, 141, 142
Bykov, Rolan, 144

C

Central Institute of Museums and Excursions (*Tsentral'nyi muzeino-ekskursionnyi institut*), 46
Chekhov, Anton, 142
Chicken Riaba, The, 137
Civilization: European, 170; grandfatherification of Soviet, 62; myth of Lenin as feature of Soviet, 13; socialist model of, 124; Soviet society as a species of, 95; Soviet, 54, 67,

69, 96, 124; Stalinist, 54; woman as bearer of, 107
Collectivism, 45
Communism: according to Berdiaev, 149; communist propaganda, 48-9; the breakdown of, 78, 169
Communist Party, the, 78, 79, 81, 82, 85, 87, 89, 119, 126, 134; -s battle against religion, 57, 83-4; and Pavlov, 54, 55, 58, 61; Central Committee of, 79, 82, 83, 84, 86, 89, 90-1; Congress 1956, 80, 81, 84, 85, 86, 91; Congress 1961, 81; german, 48; Lenin as embodiment of, 14, 27-8; under Stalin, 134
CPSU: see: Communist Party
Cruel Romance, 142
Cultural: change, 118 heritage, 161; poverty, 126; Soviet history, 41
Culture, 148, 157; alternative, 153; body, 115, 117, 118; consumer, 127-8; dissident, 154; dominant vs. oppositional, 126; formal vs. informal, 126; global, 127; of poverty, 96, 108; officially-accepted, 147, 154, 160; party, 129; peasant, 98, 99; physical, 115, 118, 119, 120, 122, 123; Russian Orthodox, 33 Russian political, 21; Russian, 34, 39, 134, 138, 144, 148; sex in Soviet, 33; Soviet ceremonial, 126; Soviet, 130, 134, 148; Stalinist, 50, 58; traditional, 104; underground, 147, 153, 154, 157; Western, 153; woman in Russian, 107

D

Darwin, 63
Descartes, 151; Cartesian dualism, 149
Dolphins: as "intellectuals of the sea", 68, 69; as the noble savage, 71; in the Red Navy, 72; matriarchal society of, 69, 71
Durkheim, Emile, 15

E

Eastern Europe, 171; transition in, 165, 170, 181; Western economic 'assistance' to, 169
Elias, Norbert, 102, 111
Erofeev, Venedikt, 153
Erofeev, Viktor, 156

F

Farewell to Matera, 135
Farewell, 135
Fear (Strakh), 58
Folklore, 99; urban, 105
Fonda, Jane, 115, 116, 131
Frank, Simon, 151-53
Freud, 14
Fromm, Erich, 16

G

Gastric juice factory, the, 60-1
Garage, The, 143
Geineke, 46

German, Aleksei, 142
German, Iurii, 142
German: Communist Party, 48, 49; communists, 48; guilds, 48; proletarians, 47; "social-democratic" tourism, 49; workers, 47-8; working class, 47
Gerner, 169
Glaubauf, 47-8
Goncharov, 159
Gor'kii, Maksim, 55, 142
Gorbachev, 144
Govorukhin, Stanislav, 139-40
Gromyko, M. M., 103

H

Hedlund, 169
Herzen, Alexander, 160
History: of peasantry, 106; Russian, 140, 144; Soviet cultural, 41; Soviet period of Russia's, 96; Soviet, 101, 122
Hitler, 108; -s Germany and Stalin's Soviet Union, 88
Huizinga, Jan, 17
Humble Cemetery, The, 154

I

I lived Revolution, 77
Ideology: Bolshevik, 144; of paternalistic materialism, 61; of socialism, 120, 167; official, 57, 156; Soviet, 58, 167; Soviet-Marxist, 120, 147
Institute of the Physiology and Pathology of Higher Nervous Activities, 56
Intelligentsia, the, 28, 77, 78, 91, 111, 119, 120, 141, 143, 149
Ivanov-Smolenskii, A., 64

K

Kabakov, Il'ia, 154-55
Kaganovich, 81
Kaledin, Sergei, 154, 157
Kalinin, 31; as 'all-Union elder', 62
Kant, Immanuel, 21
Khrushchev Remembers: The Last Testament, 77
Khrushchev, Nikita,14, 85; -s reforms, 80-1
Kleinenberg, S., 69
Kliamkin, 34
Klimov, Elem, 135, 139
Kochetov, 81
Krupskaia, 26, 34, 35
Krylenko, Nikolai, 41, 47
KSM (Communist League of Youth), 42

L

Le Bon, 14
Lenin, Vladimir Ilich, 55, 65, 85, 108; -s death, 18; -s doctrine of consciousness, 58, 71; -s human being, 63, 66 -s possible Jewishness, 31, 32, 35; -s presence in everyday life, 25, 26; -s theory of the mind, 58; -s works, 26, 27; and sex, 33-4, 35-6; as 'immortal', 16, 19-20; as a cruel figure, 35; as Anti-Christ, 19; as class symbol, 28, 30, 32; as embodiment of the Communist Party, 14, 27-8; as father-figure, 14, 20-1, 23, 24-5, 26; as martyr, 32; as national symbol, 30-32, 35;

as role model, 32, 33, 35;
as supreme judge, 20, 24;
as supreme teacher, 26-7, 34;
as the good Tsar, 14;
cult of, 13, 21, 33, 34;
myth of, 13, 21;
religious terms in reference to, 15-19; visual imagery of, 17
Lesgaft Academy of Physical Culture, 115, 116
Life with an Idiot, 156
Lilly, John C., 67
Literaturnaia gazeta, 7
Little Vera, 157
Lukacs, Georg, 158
Lunacharskii, 15
Lysenkoism, 58

M

Maiakovskii, Vladimir, 28
Mamin, Iurii, 141
Man and Dolphin, 67
Marx, 15, 19, 27, 28, 64
Marxism-Leninism, 120, 168; as a secular religion, 15, 16
Matryona's Home, 139
Memoirs, (Il'ia Kabakov), 154
Mikhalkov, Nikita, 141, 142
Mikhalkov-Konchalovskii, Andrei, 137
Mindadze, Alexander, 140, 141
Mirror, 138
Modernisation, 117, 118, 124; and the body, 117; post-Soviet form of, 126; processes of, 117, 122; Soviet model of unfinished, 131; Soviet model of, 120, 124, 125, 131
Modernity, 116-17, 119, 124, 126; civilizational devices of, 50;
Russian version of, 118, 131; Soviet Union as project of, 39; socialist model of, 124; Soviet model of unfinished, 123; unfinished, 116, 124, 125, 126, 131; Western, 117, 118, 125
Molotov, 57, 81
Monastyrskii, Andrei, 157
MOPR (the international Organisation to Assist Revolutionary Fighters), 42
Moscow-Petushki, 153
Mosse, George, 15
Muratova, Kira, 158
MVD (the Ministry of Internal Affairs), 79, 91
My Friend Ivan Lapshin, 142
My, 152

N

Na sushe i na more, 41, 43, 46, 47, 49
National identity, 133-34, 138, 144, 161, 167, 171, 180; and local reality, 176
Nationalism, 31, 167, 170; and village prose, 135; Russian, 133, 137
Nauka i zhizn', 67
Neizvestny, Ernst, 157
Nekrasov, 35
Nicholas I, 160
Nostalgia, 138
Novyi Mir, 81

O

Oblomov, 159
Oktiabr', 81
OSOAVIAKHIM (The Union of Societies of Friends for the

Index

Defence of the Aviation and Chemical Industries), 42
Ostrovskii, Alexander, 142

P

Panfilov, Gleb, 142
Pavlov, I. P.: and Stalin, 53, 54, 58, 64, 65; and the Party, 54, 55-6, 58; and Marxism, 56; cult, 58; -s likeness to Darwin and the ape, 63; and Lenin, 55-6, 58, 63, 65, 71; -s Institute, 56; as 'elder', 57, 61-2
Pavlovian: anti-Pavlovians, 55, 66, 67, 68, 69; doctrine, 56, 71; dog, 53, 55, 59, 63, 65, 66; dogma, 58; experiments and the Party's reconstruction of society, 54; indoctrination within Soviet science, 65; laboratory and Soviet society, 54, 58, 59; materialism, 57; neo-Pavlovians, 55, 65, 67-8 paradigm, 57, 68; physiology, 64; school of biology, 54-5 science, 55, 57, 58
Pavlovism, 56, 57, 65, 67; and Lysenkoism, 58; Stalinism, 71
People's Archive, The, 95
Petrenko, N., 30
Platonov, Andrei, 45
Pluralism: ethnic, 178
Popov, Evgenii, 156
Prigov, Dmitrii, 156
Pushkin, 141

R

Rasputin, Grigorii, 139
Rasputin, Valentin, 135

Religion, 149; Orthodox, 18, 33; Soviet Union as a 'secular', 14-15; the Party's battle against, 57, 83-4
Repentance, 140, 142, 157
Reswich, William, 77
Riazanov, El'dar, 142
Romanov family, the, 139
Rossiiskoe obshchestvo turistov (Russian Society of Tourists) (ROT), 46
Rubinstein, Lev, 156
Russia We Have Lost, The, 139, 144
Russia: and the West, 134, 138; Brezhnev's, 143; destiny of, 133, 144; post-revolutionary, 119; post-Soviet Russia, 8, 77, 129, 131; pre-Petrine, 149; pre-revolutionary, 8, 118, 139, 142; the fate of, 135; the new, 7, 8, 77, 91, 133, 161; transformation in, 116-7, 131; Western economic assistance to, 169;
Russian: discourse, 39; economy, 169; literature, 143; Messianism, 150; national character, 21; nationalism, 133, 137; new bourgeoisie, 128; society, 15, 80, 111, 148, 150, 160; values, 137, 141, 142

S

Sacrifice, 138, 139
Saussurean: dichotomies, 40; linguistics 40
Scarecrow, 144
Servant, The, 140
Severin, Ivor, 156
Shaginian, M., 31
Shepit'ko, Larisa, 144

Shmelev, Nikolai, 7
Shukshin, Vasilii, 135, 139
Sideburns, 141
Sitnikov, 155
Snowball Berry Red, 135, 136
Socialism: 15, 24, 80, 167, 180; 'liberal', 81; anthropology of, 167; as religion, 16; as ritualism, 68; discourse of, 81, 168; ideology of, 120, 167; Lenin as embodiment of, 27; with a 'human face', 55
Socialist realism, 134, 139, 142, 158; replaced by social realism, 7
Society of Proletarian Tourism and Excursions (*Obshchestvo proletarskogo turizma i ekskursii*) (OPTE), 41, 43, 46-7, 48-9
Solzhenitsyn, Alexander, 139, 140
Sovetskii turist, 46
Sovetskoe gosudarstvo i pravo, 79
Soviet Political Mind, The, 53
Soviet society, 53, 95, 101, 103, 110, 111, 123, 174; and the Pavlovian laboratory, 58; as a dichotomic one, 148, 166, 167; as product of Modern cultural history, 39; consumption in, 124, 127; culture and consciousness in, 148, 157; dissent within, 78, 85; horizontal communication in, 91: of the 1930s, 148; post-Soviet, 115, 116, 178; state and, 78, 80, 91; under Khrushchev, 80-81, 91; under Stalin, 124; vs. the individual, 149, 155
Soviet: anti-Soviet activity, 82, 84, 85, 86, 89; development, 125; discourse, 55; elites, 127; everyday life, 41, 102, 129, 155; man, 68; power, 15, 79; propaganda, 18, 27; psychology, 53; reality, 45, 148, 155; science, 65; Soviet-Marxist ideology, 147, 151; sport, 115, 120, 123; system, 90, 91, 167; transition, 166
Spiritual Foundations of Society, The, 152
Stalin, 31, 53, 54, 57, 80, 108, 111, 133; -s camps, 16; -s decree of man, 64, 65; -s doctrine of consciousness, 58; -s Soviet Union and Hitlers Germany, 88; -s works, 27; cult of, 13, 21; de-stalinization, 55; demonic image of, 14; Khrushchev unmasking, 81; naming of, 25; period, 58, 83, 140; reign of, 77; the Party under, 134
Stalinism, 16, 40, 80; discourse of, 63, 66
Stalinist: civilization, 54; culture, 50, 58; ideology, 56; society, 40, 53-4; terror, 140, 141; tourism, 40, 41, 49; tradition, 81
Stalker, 141
Steinberg, Erik, 155
Stolypin, 140
Svobodnaia Evropa (Radio Free Europe), 87

T

Tarde, 14
Tarkovskii, Andrei, 138, 139, 141

Tereshkova, Valentina, 109
Thaw, the, 78, 153; Soviet science during, 65
To Kill A Dragon, 140
Ton, Konstantin, 160
Tourism, 41; as civilising device, 49-50; as instrument of the Party, 43, 49; educational, 46, 49: German "social-democratic", 49; history of, 46; pre-Revolutionary, 45, 46, 47; principles of, 46; stalinist, 40, 41, 49; Western commercial, 47
Traditional, custom, 106; the collapse of values, 104, 105
Trotskii, 19
Trubetskoi, Evgenii, 150
Tsar Alexander III, 111
Tsipko, 34
Tucker, Robert C., 53
Tvardovskii, 81

U

Ul'ianova, A. I., 31
Ulianov's Family, 31

Uncle Mazai, 35
Unfinished Piece for Mechanical Piano, 142

V

Valentinov, N., 24, 26-7
Vassa Zheleznova, 142
Vassa, 142
Vavilov, S. I., 58
Voronin, L. G., 65, 67

W

Westernization, 180, 181
What Is To Be Done?, 19

Y

Yablokov, Aleksei, V. 68, 69
Yagoda, 77
Yeltsyn, 68

Z

Zakharov, Mark, 140, 141
Zamiatin, 152
Zaslavskii, 90
Zinov'ev, Grigorii, 19, 27, 28, 33